D1540296

Embraced

Embraced

Prodigals at the Cross

STEVE SHERWOOD

Foreword by Leonard Sweet

WIPF & STOCK · Eugene, Oregon

Wipf & Stock
An Imprint of Wipf and Stock Publishers
199 W. 8th Ave., Suite 3
Eugene, OR 97401

www.wipfandstock.com

ISBN 13: 978-1-60899-107-5

Manufactured in the U.S.A.

Permissions:
Crying Out used by permission of Kelsey Vanden Hoek.

Harvest used by permission of Tim Timmerman.

I Was Afraid Because I Was Naked, So I Hid and *The Banquet/The Heart Party*
used by permission of Andrew Watson.

Lyrics from "Good Advice" from the album *Only the Bony* used by permission of
J. J. Alberhasky.

Rachel and Dad; *The Heart Party*; and *J. J., Bailey, and Rachel at the Heart Party* used
by permission of Elizabeth Sherwood.

St. John's Cross used by permission of David Sherwood.

The Three used by permission of Meghan Hedley.

All scripture references are from *Today's New International Version* (TNIV).
Copyright © 2005 by Zondervan. Used by permission of Zondervan,
www.zondervan.com.

To my wife, Elizabeth,
and our daughters, Bailey and Rachel,
living examples of steadfast love.
Together, you are a place of shalom for me.

I will arise and go to Jesus,

He will embrace me in his arms,

In the arms of my dear savior,

Oh, there are ten thousand charms.

—*Appalachian folk hymn*

Contents

Contents

Contents

Illustrations

Foreword

CHRISTIANS HAVE A MODEST and humble ambition: We want to save the world.

The March 4, 2002, cover of *Time* magazine had a photo of Bono on it with the caption, "Can Bono Save the World?" First, the answer is "No." Bono cannot "save the world." Only Jesus can do that. Second, Bono can change the world, but the world is hungry for salvation, not just change.

The name *Jesus* means exactly who he is: God saves. Jesus is the God who saves. The ancient question *cur Deus homo?* or "Why did God become man?" is answered in this gospel song I grew up singing in Holiness camp meetings:

> We have heard the joyful sound:
> Jesus saves! Jesus saves!
> Spread the tidings all around:
> Jesus saves! Jesus saves!
> Bear the news to ev'ry land,
> Climb the steeps and cross the waves;
> Onward! 'tis our Lord's command;
> Jesus saves! Jesus saves![1]

The answer to *cur Deus homo?* was given less lustily in the Nicene Creed: "for us and for our salvation."

If the mission of Jesus is the redemption of the human race, then Jesus' death on a cross becomes of universal significance and deep theological importance. The greatest Anglican theologian of the twentieth century, Austin Farrer, spent six pages probing this one line from Mrs. Alexander's famous hymn: "There was no other good enough to pay the price of sin."[2] If you believe "Jesus Saves," you take what happened on the cross seriously. At least Christianity's first converts did. The first two members of the "church," the thief and the centurion, came to faith

1. Owens, "Jesus Saves."
2. Alexander, "There Is a Green Hill Far Away."

from the crucifixion, *not* the resurrection. Christianity without the atonement is more than Christmas without Bing Crosby or Nat King Cole. It's Christianity without Christmas.

"Somehow," Jesus bore the evil of the world in his body on that tree. As C. S. Lewis put it, "The central Christian belief is that Christ's death has somehow put us right with God and given us a fresh start . . . A good many different theories have been held as to how it works; what all Christians agree on is that it does work."[3]

Two of the most famous theories of how it "works" were elaborated in their classic forms by two contemporaries: Anselm and Abelard. Anselm was Archbishop of Canterbury at the end of the eleventh century when he wrote a book titled *Cur Deus Homo*, or "Why God Became Man." His answer was that God's justice required that sin be punished. But instead of the death of the sinner, God provides a substitute, and in the sacrifice of God's only Son, Jesus paid the price. Anselm said that "only a human word, a human act" can repair human history, while "only the divine freedom is adequate to bring this about." In a world where many people were slaves, servants, or "free" people bound by poverty and disease, the ransom view was liberating.

Peter Abelard, a younger contemporary of Anselm, was a priest and teacher at the Cathedral of Notre Dame. His view of the cross was that Jesus came to show us God's love and inspire our love. The cross more changes our hearts than God's mind. For Anselm, the crucifixion was a performance ritual with God as the audience. For Abelard, the crucifixion was a participation ritual with humans as the audience and you and me as the participants. What happened to Jesus happened to us.

Both positions have been easy targets for those within ("cosmic child abuse"[4]—Steve Chalke) and without ("that loathsome system of torture-worship"[5]—William Empson) the Christian tradition. But who would sacrifice any of our hymnody and liturgy, where you can find both Anselm and Abelard not battling it out so much as bringing different aspects of the cross into view? J. W. Alexander's lyrics in "O Sacred Head Now Wounded" convey Anselm's view:

---

3. Lewis, *Mere Christianity*, 54.

4. Chalke, *The Lost Message of Jesus*, 182.

5. Empson, quoted by Griffiths, "William Empson's Fixated Faith," paragraph 5.

What Thou, my Lord, has suffered
Was all for sinners' gain;
Mine, mine was the transgression,
But Thine the deadly pain.[6]

For Abelard's position in musical form, see Isaac Watts's hymn "When I Survey the Wondrous Cross":

Were the whole realm of nature mine,
That were an offering far too small;
Love so amazing, so Divine
Demands my soul, my life, my all.[7]

The book you have in your hands is a book about the cross of Jesus. It may not seem so at times, since Steve Sherwood doesn't really start talking directly about the cross until the last chapter. But *Embraced: Prodigals at the Cross* is a moving and profound meditation on the meaning of the cross from almost every tip of the crossbars. Each angle on the atonement is a piece of the atonement mosaic, and—what is most refreshing—artists, poets, musicians, and filmmakers get a chance to add their prowess and perspectives to the mosaic.

One of the rarest and richest features of this book is the way its author lingers in the Hebrew Scriptures, adding nuance and fullness to his culminating understanding of the cross. Don't be fooled by the author's breezy, conversational style and glide over the depths of the insights. For example, Steve has provided his readers with the best discussion of the Hebrew word *hesed* I've seen in English.

The author has also countered Descartes with the best riposte to "I think, therefore I am." For Sherwood, the Christian version goes like this: "I relate, therefore I am."

Leonard Sweet
Drew University, George Fox University
sermons.com

---

6. Alexander, "O Sacred Head Now Wounded."
7. Watts, "When I Survey the Wondrous Cross."

Preface

THIS BOOK HAS BEEN stewing inside of me for a long time. When I was sixteen years old, I sat in a living room in Round Rock, Texas, at a Young Life[1] meeting and heard a college student tell the story of Hosea and Gomer and then say, "God loves us like that." I'd never heard anything like that, and I now know that Hosea was *not* a story regularly told in Young Life. I have no idea why my Young Life leader chose it. Regardless, that image has stuck in my mind for almost thirty years.

Other experiences and stories along the way—from my ministry, my personal life, my family life, or books I have read—have lodged themselves in my mind as well. Together they have formed a sort of stew brewing in my head and my heart. This book is an attempt to communicate what has come from all of that.

Just as the message about Jesus' love being like Hosea's for Gomer came to me through a told story with very little additional comment, I hope you'll find this to be mostly a storytelling book. I will comment here and there, but as often as possible, I hope to get out of the way and let the stories, from both the Bible and elsewhere, speak for themselves. Also, I will not try to connect every story to the next in hopes that together they will create a similar stew for you, one that marinates and coalesces into the most compelling story of all: the story of God's great love for you.

1. Young Life is an international, interdenominational Christian ministry to middle-school and high-school students. It is almost seventy years old, with branches in communities all across the United States and around the world.

Acknowledgments

IT IS IMPOSSIBLE TO adequately thank all the people who have contributed to this book in one way or another. My parents, David and Carol Sherwood, nurtured me into faith from an early age and gave me a love for stories. My wife, Elizabeth, and our daughters, Bailey and Rachel, love me and have been infinitely patient in the months it took for this project to come together. My brother, Jonathon, with his blend of loving support and honestly skeptical questioning, has been a great blessing.

Over the years, ideas and stories have come into my life from many diverse and wonderful sources: from professors such as Ray Anderson and Terry McGonigal at Fuller Theological Seminary and Larry Shelton and Len Sweet at George Fox Evangelical Seminary; from authors and thinkers such as C. S. Lewis, Frederick Buechner, Walker Percy, Miroslav Volf, and T. F. Torrance; from colleagues and friends in ministry and teaching, such as Bob Davidson, J. J. and Ellie Alberhasky, Jon and Annie Houghton, Matt Browning, Mike Love, and many, many more; from students and Young Life kids from Massachusetts to Iowa and, finally, George Fox University in Oregon; from musicians ranging from U2 to Bruce Cockburn and Bruce Springsteen.

The images that begin, and in some cases end, each part are of two sorts. Some are photos that are either of an event discussed in the preceding part or that somehow evoke the part that follows. The artwork is by three George Fox University students and a faculty member in the George Fox Art Department, each in response to one or more of the themes discussed in its accompanying part of the book or representing one of its themes. The artists' names are Tim Timmerman, MFA; Andrew Watson; Meghan Hedley; and Kelsey Vanden Hoek. My belief is that we convey meaning and ideas as powerfully, if not more so, in image as we do in word. My hope is that these images evoke meaning and enhance your interaction with the ideas and stories of the book.

Acknowledgments

I owe an incalculable debt to Gail Ebersole, a friend and patron for almost twenty years, who has encouraged me and opened doors for ministry and growth at every turn in the road. You are a great woman and a great leader.

An additional debt is owed to Karen Nichols, who has patiently borne with my sloppy manuscript and inability to follow even the simplest instructions. You are a great and gentle editor.

Finally, I am infinitely grateful to Gary Fowler, who, as a college student in 1979, gave a Young Life talk about Hosea and Gomer and got this whole thing started.

To all of you, thank you.

INTRODUCTION

Where Are We Going?

Harvest by Tim Timmerman

B EFORE EXPLAINING A BIT about how this book will be laid out and what it will try to cover, I'd like to share a story. I don't come out too well in this story, but I think it is one that helps frame why I want to take the approach I will take in this book and why I hope this book might be useful to others.

AGAINST FORMULIZING THE GOSPEL

We all have moments we are proud of and plenty of moments we are not. In a couple of decades of youth ministry, I've had a fair number of the former and more than enough of the latter. One of my most I-wince-when-I-think-about-it moments has also been one of the most paradigm changing. If a paradigm is the mental picture we use to make sense of the world around us, the paradigm I had as I sat on the lawn of a Young Life camp in the Catskills of New York in 1988 was pretty cut and dried. I had a very clear picture of who was a Christian and who was not and, also, a very clear picture of how one moved from being one to the other. Joining me on that lawn that afternoon was a high school freshman, John.

John and had come to Young Life in his town of Catonsville, Maryland, the previous fall, and I was one of his leaders. John and I had hit it off immediately. He was an incredibly nice, enthusiastic, and guileless young man. For reasons beyond my understanding, John thought I hung the moon. He never missed any Young Life event I attended, always wanted me to give him a ride home, and called several times to make sure he'd be in my cabin at camp that summer. All week long, John hung on every word I said at night in the cabin and wanted to hang out all afternoon at the waterfront and around camp.

Our conversation on the lawn that day was more intentional than most. It was late in the week, and I was having thirty-minute conversations with every guy in the cabin, asking how they'd enjoyed the week and attempting to "close the deal" in a conversion sense. We'd all heard a week of talks laying out the Gospel, and this was an opportunity to answer any questions they might have and to ask them the all-important question, "Would you like to give your life to Christ right now?" I was sure John was going to be an enthusiastic, "Yes!"

An hour and a half into our conversation, things weren't going as well as I'd planned. The hang-up was that John was Lutheran. Not that there is any problem with being a Lutheran. It just meant that when I asked him if he wanted to make a commitment to Christ, he said, "I don't know what you mean. I was raised Lutheran. I've always been a Christian."

My response was, "Sure. And that's super. But have you ever specifically confessed your sins and prayed for God to forgive you and accepted the work Jesus did in dying for you on the cross and asked him into your heart?"

To which he responded, "No, but I believe all of that and I think Jesus has been in my heart most all of my life."

I didn't want to be condescending or insult his family, his church, or his view of his past, but I really needed to get through to him that, while it was great to go to church all his life and all, he really wasn't a Christian yet. I told him that I could spend my whole life in a garage and that wouldn't make me a car. I could spend every weekend attending weddings and that wouldn't make me married. I used every possible illustration I could think of to make the point that no amount of family or personal church involvement was adequate if he did not have a specific moment where he prayed the "Sinner's Prayer."

Finally, literally with tears welling up in his eyes, John asked me if I thought that he'd go to hell if he died right then because he'd not prayed the prayer I'd been suggesting for over an hour that he pray. I said, "I'm really sorry to say this, John, but yes, that is what would happen." He said he'd like to stop talking and walked off back to the cabin alone.

Later that evening, John stood up along with a hundred or so other kids in camp and said that that afternoon he had become a Christian. I'd won. And I felt terrible.

Now, I want to be clear: No one in Young Life told me that I needed to browbeat John like that, nor do I want to suggest that the other kids who stood up did so under the kind of pressure that John did. I pressured John on my own. I also want to be clear that I think thousands upon thousands of folks *do* come to faith in very specific moments of conversion and, even, that a lot of folks who grow up going to church don't really believe any of it or have any experience of the grace of the Gospel. Those were reasons I used to convince myself that I'd done the right thing.

What I knew in my heart, though, was that those things weren't true about John. He had heard the Gospel and believed it in his church and in his home growing up. He didn't have a conversion moment, but he had faith all the same. He just didn't fit into my box, my clearly prescribed method of joining the Christian team. He said the prayer I asked him to, because he loved me and because I'd literally scared the hell out of him. But I had a sinking feeling that it was I who needed to repent that afternoon, not John.

I needed to repent of not thinking God could work in John's life in any way other than the formula I knew. I needed to repent of disrespecting his family and his church. Mostly, I needed to repent of not meeting him on that lawn, person-to-person, and listening to and understanding him and his life. Without recognizing it, I had turned John into a cog in my machine of conversion. I'd dehumanized him. I'd turned him into an "it" to be manipulated. Because he loved me, he let me, and that just made it all the worse.

Now, I again want to say that many people have moments of profound conversion. The apostle Paul, in the book of Acts, is a prime example. In a moment, on the road to Damascus, he is confronted by a vision of the risen Jesus and goes from being a violent persecutor of followers of Jesus to one of his greatest champions. Many people, to this day, can describe similarly vivid experiences of change.

At the same time, a close read of the Gospels shows that people "respond to Jesus" in literally dozens of different ways. Peter followed him for months and years before publicly stating his belief in Jesus as Lord and even then gets a good bit of it wrong. The thief on the cross does nothing more than make the request, "Jesus, remember me when you come into your Kingdom" and is told that salvation is his.

All of this is to say that we make mistakes when we overly systemize how someone comes to faith. Over the last century, several very easy to remember and communicate evangelism tools have emerged: the Four Spiritual Laws, the Sinner's Prayer, the Roman's Road, to name just a few. The organization I work for, Young Life, has a very clear, logical seven-day talk progression for leading kids to response at camp. All of these tools have things that recommend them and boast thousands of people who have found them to be keys to their conversions. My suggestion, however, is that when a tool becomes confused with the very reality of conversion, a great mistake has been made. That was the mistake I tragically made on that lawn with John. Rather than seeing that his experience didn't fit my "tool" and, therefore, listening genuinely to him, I thought my tool was absolutely essential. I thought it was conversion itself.

A large portion of this book will look at the spiritual realities that lie behind these formulas. In the process, I hope we will find the Gospel to be both less simple and even more beautiful than we've previously thought or imagined.

WHAT'S IN A STORY?

When I was in graduate school, a professor made this comment about analyzing things: "What's the greatest problem with dissecting an animal to get at what's inside? You have to kill it first." What was his point? That sometimes when we approach big ideas, or big texts (like the Bible), our approach to "understanding" them is to break the ideas down, study them, analyze them, and produce books summarizing every facet of them. We can learn real things that way, but first we have to kill the idea, the text.

Have you ever watched a movie, read a book, or heard a song that gets in your mind and haunts you for days afterward? I had a friend who had taken a lot of film classes in college. I hated going to movies with him. The second we'd leave a movie, he would launch into a detailed analysis of the director's choice of film, the pacing of the scene transitions, or the nuances of camera angles. He saw every part of every film. *And he missed the whole thing!* All he could see were the hundreds of parts. He couldn't see the story. The story is what has life. The story is what gets in our heads and keeps haunting us.

I grew up in a church that was very plain. We were very suspicious of churches that had statues all over the place or a lot of huge paintings of Jesus on the walls. We didn't worship "idols"; we worshipped God. And in our smugness, we missed out on quite a lot. For two thousand years, some Christian traditions have valued *icons*, which are much different from the *idols* we accused them of worshipping. Here's the difference: An idol *is* the god; I look to it and say, "This is God." An icon is a window to a point beyond. It is a hint at something that can't be contained in a particular image. No maker of an icon would say, "This is God." They would say something like, "This is just to get your mind and heart to God, to point the way to something beyond." A good image, metaphor, or story serves as an icon, pointing the way or ushering us into a larger truth, a larger world. The image or metaphor, no matter how useful, should never be confused for the thing itself.

Sometimes, the bigger the idea or the truth to be considered, the more we need to fight the temptation to turn on our scientific, logical, analytic brains and instead sit back like a moviegoer in a theater and let the lights go down and the story wash over us. A neurologist might be able to tell you what exact brain functions are happening and in what or-der when you "fall in love," but that doesn't get at the *real thing*. To do that, you've got to experience it, live it, let love touch you. All of the scientific explanations might help you a bit, but if we think they explain all there is to love, we've turned them into idols. We sometimes do that with our theology. "Here is how God works." "This is what Jesus accomplished on the cross." That kind of talk can, at times, be dangerous. If we are not careful, if we hold our pronouncements too tightly, we have turned our theology into an idol. We begin to feel that our description of the thing, or our understanding of what we take to be scripture's meaning, is the sum total of the entire thing. It is only helpful when it remains an icon, when it points us to something bigger, more mysterious, and more wonderful than our best ideas and words can describe. Our metaphors and categories may be helpful and faithful to scripture, but, given the vastness of the ideas they seek to illumine, they will always be incomplete. We need to keep in mind that at best they are icons.

The brilliant twentieth-century British author C. S. Lewis wrote two books about pain. He wrote the first, *The Problem of Pain,* when he was a bachelor. It is a brilliant and thorough intellectual consideration of how a Christian could make sense of a universe in which pain and a loving God both exist. The second book, *A Grief Observed,* was written late in his life and consists of excerpts of his diary from the twelve months immediately following the death of his beloved wife, Joy. The two books could not be more different. The Lewis of the latter book has none of the confidence and certainty that the Lewis of the first had. Instead, the reader finds a Lewis wrestling with doubt, anger, and pain in a profoundly human way, much like the rest of us do. Theologians for decades have found *The Problem of Pain* to be a useful text, a helpful intellectual exercise. People who have suffered great loss and are desperate for comfort have turned again and again to *A Grief Observed.*

The difference between these two approaches is what I'd like to explore with this book. As a Christian, I believe that absolutely nothing in the world is more important than the fact that, two thousand or so years ago, Jesus Christ was born, lived, died on a cross, and rose from the dead. Thousands upon thousands of pages of theology have been written trying to nail down what all of that meant, and I certainly couldn't hope to improve upon all of that. I would like, however, to tell those stories, and a few others, in a way that might make some sense of what it means to live with and interact with the story of Jesus. So, while there might be a theological comment here or there in the pages that follow, I hope you mostly encounter stories or images that provide doors or windows that point beyond to something bigger and more profound. To that end, none of them are meant to be the final word. Some may not work for you at all. But my hope is that, by the end, you'll somewhere along the way feel drawn into this story, this event, this person that has captivated humanity for two millennia—Jesus.

I have divided the text into four parts that suggest a narrative progression. I begin by suggesting that we were created as relational beings by an inherently relational God, and that this was a beautiful and wonderful thing. Tragically, however, things have gone horribly wrong, and the Bible is the story of how that happened and how God responds. That story climaxes in the life, death, and resurrection of Jesus. Finally, as a result of that climax, we are put back into right relationship with God, ourselves, and one another. Within each part, the ideas are much more loosely organized. For example, in discussing sin, I do not worry about which comes first, our perpetuating sin or our experiencing the results of it. I will leave that to you to prioritize if you feel the need to do so. Personally, both realities seem to bear upon my existence daily, and I leave it at that. I'm not laying out an ordered, four-course meal within each part, but rather am setting some food out on the table for you to pick and choose from or, better yet, to throw everything into a pot to let stew. Finally, while some of the essays drive to a concluding point, many do not. This also is intentional. Going back to the image of killing an idea in order to dissect it, I want to allow most of the essays and the stories or metaphors contained in them to have a life of their own, to work on and in you in their own way. My fear is that if I summed up each essay with a couple of easy, memorable points, I would be stunting the power of the metaphor to speak for itself. My hope is that the story will go on speaking to you as you ruminate on it, and that this will go beyond any summary or conclusion I could draw for you.

PART ONE

Who We Are and What We Were Made For

*W*HAT DID GOD HAVE *in mind for humanity, for you and me, when God first created us? Much as parents daydream of possibilities as they await their first child, what was the life God intended for all of us? It doesn't take much looking at the world or in our own hearts to quickly conclude that the world is profoundly screwed up. Was there ever a time when things weren't like this? Is this all there is? Is this the best we can hope for, or is there something more?*

The biblical idea for this "something more" is shalom. Shalom is a wonderfully roomy word, a concept with wide arms that can take in much more than just Jesus coming to deal with my guilt before God. It can encompass Jesus coming to deal with, literally, everything that is wrong and broken in our world. It's a word with a great past and, I believe, an even better future.

Key to understanding what we were made for is grasping who we are and where we came from. To that end, let's take some time to consider what kind of God created us and what it means to suggest that, somehow, we were made in that God's image.

Rachel and Dad, Oregon Coast, 2005

The Great Banquet Comes to Texas

Entering high school in Round Rock, Texas, at a large school and having just moved to town from out of state, I felt completely anonymous. In halls packed with hundreds of other kids, I felt totally alone. I was not a troubled kid. I got good grades, did reasonably well in sports, and really enjoyed being in the band. My parents were together, and I knew they loved me. But none of that, particularly in the first months of school, helped take away my loneliness. That fall, I had two experiences, one that deeply heightened my sense of isolation and another that helped wash the pain of it away.

Both experiences involved my participation on the cross-country team. Partway through the season, due to a couple of injuries to better, faster runners, I found myself on the varsity team—the seventh man on the seven-man varsity.

Every Friday (meets were on Saturday mornings), the team would have a light workout, just a few miles, mostly run around the large high school campus. The varsity always ran together in a group. Since I was the new kid in the group, the other six told me they'd fill me in on how it worked. We would be running three laps around the campus, including a pass by the school's cafeteria with what seemed like one hundred yards of glass windows. Being a Friday afternoon in Texas, the cafeteria would be busy with cheerleaders making banners for that night's football game and the drill team going through their dance routine a few last times. Every time we ran by, we would do something to get their attention.

I was a little nervous, but that was okay. I'd just follow my teammates' lead. On the first lap, we all would dance and sing the school fight song. We did. A few of the girls in the cafeteria, the coolest girls in the school, looked up, but we were just the emaciated, geeky cross-country guys, so we didn't get much attention. On the next pass, they said that, since it was my first time on varsity, they'd all put me on their shoulders and run by carrying me. They did, and it was pretty cool. More folks noticed us this time, and I felt awesome. I was excited to see what would top this on the final lap.

Well, the last pass was quite a bit different. As we got halfway in front of the glass windows, the other guys all tackled me. And took my clothes off. Within seconds, I was in front of a window of the most intimidating girls in the school, all of whom were paying attention this time, and I was stripped down to nothing but my underwear. Then the other guys ran off. I sat there for what seemed like an eternity, trying to hide myself. I felt desperately alone and exposed.

It was one of the most horrific moments of my adolescent life.

While a great deal more intense than my daily experience, this moment was much like how I felt all the time at that point in my life. I was a skinny, shy, and awkward kid in the halls of a 2,000-student high school. I desperately wanted both to be noticed in a meaningful way *and* to hide at the same time. I was alone and afraid pretty much every day.

My other experience of that fall could not have been more different. The girl across the street, who was a year older than me and whom I thought was kind of cute, had invited me to a Young Life meeting. If 200 kids came, the leader was going to swallow a live goldfish or something like that. I didn't know what Young Life was, but it sure beat staying home alone, which was how I pretty much spent every evening.

I didn't really like the meeting that much. It was loud and hot, and I didn't really know who to talk to. I wasn't all that sold on ever going back. During the evening, a University of Texas student named Gary Fowler came up to me and introduced himself. He asked me what kinds of activities I did at school. He seemed kind of awkward. I didn't think twice about it.

Over the next several weeks, Gary started showing up at all of my cross-country meets. These weren't all local. They were sometimes an hour or more away from town and were rather early on Saturday mornings. He'd always stop by our team camp, say hello, and talk to me for a couple of minutes, and that would be it.

After a month of this, I asked him, "So, Gary, why do you come to all our meets? To watch Eddie Martinez?" (Martinez was the senior on our team who'd placed third in state the year before.)

"No," Gary replied. "I've heard of him and he's pretty awesome, but not really."

"You must have run in high school, then. You must just really love the sport."

"Actually, I've never run at all. In high school, I did gymnastics" (maybe the only sport in Texas less cool for a guy to participate in than mine!).

"So, what in the world are you doing here?"

"Well, Steve. I met you at that Young Life meeting a few weeks back, and you said you ran cross-country, and I figured coming to your meets would be a way to get to know you, so I went by the school and got a schedule."

Over the remainder of my time at Round Rock, I spent hours upon hours with Gary. We went out for pizza. He invited me to a Bible study with a bunch of kids from my school, and many of them became my best friends. Gary gave me rides everywhere.

Of the half-dozen college kids that composed the Young Life leadership team at Round Rock High, Gary was probably the least cool. He'd done gymnastics in high school, after all—maybe the only sport a guy could play in football-crazed Texas that had less prestige than cross-country. He drove a tiny, beat-up car with nothing but an AM radio. When he led music at Young Life, he was hopelessly off key. None of that mattered to me. Gary was the one who showed up at my cross-country meets.

Jesus told a story that, though wildly different in its details, in many ways perfectly describes both of my experiences of that fall. Over and over, Jesus used the image of parties or banquets to describe what he was about. He seemed to be profoundly interested in celebrating and inviting others to join in, particularly the lonely and outcast. In Luke 14, Jesus told one of his most poignant banquet stories. I'm going to take some imaginative liberties in framing and telling the narrative, but I hope you'll feel I'm true to the heart of the story Jesus told.

The story begins, "A certain man was preparing a great banquet and invited many guests . . ."

Time Out for Historical Context

KNOWING THAT JESUS OFTEN participated in or told stories about parties or banquets, one is left to wonder, why? Why does he choose an image of a celebratory meal to explain what he is about? Is there some history here that we need to know about? From the very beginning, the life of Israel had been liberally sprinkled with times of celebration. It has sometimes been tempting for Christians to look at the Old Testament and primarily see rules, laws, and judgment. That is a great mistake. At Mount Sinai, just after the Israelites escaped slavery in Egypt and at the same time that God gives the Law to Moses, God also outlines the celebratory life of Israel. Throughout the year, the Israelites were to practice various celebrations for harvests, for remembering the Exodus, and for thanking God for forgiveness. All of these were warm-ups for the real deals, however.

Two of the great celebrations of Israel were to be the Sabbath Year and the Year of Jubilee, the granddaddy of all celebrations. The Sabbath Year was to be practiced every seven years and the Year of Jubilee every fifty. The Sabbath Year was to be a yearlong version of the weekly Sabbath. It was a time to rest, celebrate, and give thanks. Farmers were not to plant but give the ground a year to rest and rejuvenate (a practice that every farmer today knows is essential to soil health). In fact, the whole nation was to stop from its labor. How would they eat? How would they survive? God promised that if they practiced this year of rest, they would be blessed with such abundant harvests in the sixth year that they would have more than enough to tide them over.

The Year of Jubilee was to be even better. This year included rest from labor, but it also included much more. At this time in the history of Israel, if persons found themselves in debt that they could not pay back, they could sell themselves as slaves. One practice of the Year of Jubilee was that people in this state were to have their debts wiped away, and they were to go free. Additionally, during the course of fifty years, some families would have gotten rich and prospered while others would have struggled. In the Midwest today, small family farms are getting bought out by large corporate farms or by developers to build subdivisions. The same was true back then, except, every fifty years, the original families were to get the family land back. It was all right to amass great wealth by buying your neighbor's land for forty-nine years, but at fifty, it was time to give it back. People got a new start. The book of Leviticus summarizes this year of celebration in this way:

> I will send rain in its season, and the ground will yield its crops and the trees their fruit . . . and you will eat all the food you want and live in safety in your land. I will grant peace in the land and you will lie down and no one will make you afraid . . . You will still be eating last year's harvest when you will have to move it out to make room for the new. I will put my dwelling place among you, and I will not abhor you. I will walk among you and be your God, and you will be my people.[1]

What a great promise! The tragedy is, however, that most biblical scholars agree that Israel *never* practiced the Year of Jubilee. How could this be? Why would a people pass up this great year of blessing? Think about it: What is the key to initiating the whole process? Trusting God to take care of them. Not relying on their own wealth and power to get them through, but with open hands giving things away to others, trusting that God would fill their now empty hands with blessing. That's hard to do. Would we be any different?

1. Leviticus 26:4–12.

Back to the Story

WHEN THE JEWISH JESUS speaks of "a certain man throwing a great banquet" to his Jewish audience, this long history of anticipated Jubilee celebration would come to their minds. The banquet he is talking about is God's celebration of Jubilee, of Israel experiencing the fullness of God's shalom. The feast of the kingdom of God is the final and ultimate experience of God's blessing for all. Jesus is telling them what it's going to look like.

You can just picture "a certain man was preparing a great banquet." The great man (the image still works with a woman) quickly moving through his mansion, talking to the cooks ("No, more shrimp, a lot more. Double that. And not the cheap stuff, the very best.") while also talking on his cell phone to the musicians ("Absolutely. I want a string quartet for the patio, somebody on the grand piano in the living room . . ."). This is going to be the party to end all parties.

But in Jesus' story, the initially invited guests are hesitant to come. They don't say no, exactly, but they're distracted by other things. As the servants of the master go out to tell people the party is ready, they start making excuses. "I just bought a new team of oxen. I've got to make sure they're all settled," or "Well, I just got married, and you know how it is. I don't think I can make it."

The master is frustrated, but undeterred. He tells his employees, "Go out quickly into the streets and alleys of the town and bring in the poor, the crippled, the blind, and the lame." I absolutely love this part of the story. Try to imagine yourself as one of the poor and homeless of the town. Up pulls the master's servants: "Hey, do you want a free dinner? I can take you to a great one."

"Sure. I'm always up for a meal and a ride to boot." You pile in the car and begin to make your way across town. You near the local Catholic soup kitchen, and you're sure the car is going to pull over and let you out, but it doesn't slow down and just drives on by.

Now you're in parts of town you've never seen. The houses are getting bigger, the streets are lined with trees. As the road winds up the hill, the houses get fewer but more and more spectacular. Finally, you see the biggest house you've ever seen. What in the world is going on? The driver seems to be heading there.

You get it. The owner is throwing a party and needs some extra help. You'll pull around back to the service entrance and, for a little dishwashing or table busing, you'll be repaid with a meal. Not a bad deal at all. You're up for that. Except, the car pulls right up front.

You nervously pile out and stand awkwardly, not knowing what to do next. The front door opens and out walks the owner of the house. You vaguely recognize the face; you've seen it on TV and in the papers. He rushes up to you.

Strangely, he seems to know your name. "It's you! I'm so glad you've come. Come right in. I've got a seat with your name on it. You are going to have such a great time!"

I was not homeless or literally huddled in a back alleyway by a dumpster, but as a freshman walking anonymously through the halls of a massive high school, I felt that way. Certainly, huddling in the school parking lot, being stared at and laughed at by the beautiful, cool girls of the school, I felt that way.

And yet, someone found me. In showing up at my meets, driving me to Young Life events, and introducing me to a world of leaders and high school kids who would welcome me and love me in the name of Jesus, Gary was like the master's servants in this story. There was a place at the banquet for me.

There is a place there for all of us.

What are the implications of this story? In some very real ways, all of us are as alone as I felt that afternoon on the sidewalk outside of Round Rock High. We feel adrift from one another, and more important, we feel alienated from God. Even more important, however, is that God seeks after all of us. I believe this story told by Jesus a couple thousand years ago hints at the greatest truth in all the world: that we are loved by God, sought after by God, and invited by God to participate in the Great Banquet. The life of Jesus, from his birth to the cross and his resurrection, is the key to that invitation.

Sea World and Frederick Buechner

I N H I S B O O K, *The Longing for Home,*[1] Frederick Buechner tells a story about watching the dolphin show at Sea World in Orlando, Florida. He describes sitting there with his wife and one of his daughters as the show moves to its finale. Music soars, a dozen dolphins are doing synchronized flips all around the tank, and brightly colored parakeets soar through the scene at just the right moment. All of this occurs against the backdrop of a brilliantly blue Florida sky and a deliciously warm, but not hot, spring breeze. What makes the story striking is that Buechner reports turning to his wife and daughter and realizing that all three of them are simultaneously laughing and crying.

Anyone who has read the works of this bookish, introverted resident of a secluded farm in rural Vermont will be confused by trying to picture him sitting with the throng of tourists at Sea World in the first place. And why the tears? Buechner describes it as a moment of experiencing communion. In spite of the fact that the performance was staged and would be repeated identically a couple of hours later for another over-priced ticket paying audience, in that moment, everything in the world seemed to be in communion. The sky, the breeze, the dolphins, their trainers, the birds, Buechner, his family, and God all were at peace in that moment. Shalom happens at Sea World.

I read this little story over a decade ago and thought it interesting and then didn't think of it again for the intervening decade. And then my wife and I took our two daughters, aged seven and five, to Disneyworld and Sea World last January. On a brilliantly blue, warm but not hot morning, we found ourselves sitting at the dolphin show at Sea World. As the show reached its climax, one just like Buechner had described, I turned to my wife, Elizabeth, and we were both smiling ear to ear and crying! I remembered Buechner's story at that moment and thought, "That's just too much." But it really was a beautiful, stirring scene.

In a great, easy-to-read book, *Simply Christian,*[2] British biblical scholar N. T. Wright talks about four echoes of God in the world that cause

---

1. Buechner, *The Longing for Home,* 126–28.
2. Wright, *Simply Christian,* 39–52.

us to ache for God. One of those echoes is the presence of beauty and our hearts' yearning for it. If the world were random, there'd be no need for it to be beautiful. There'd certainly be no reason that we, as randomly constituted organisms, would have a hunger for beauty. But we do.

C. S. Lewis, in his autobiography *Surprised by Joy*,[3] describes the same phenomenon in his own pre-Christian life: moments of piercing joy in beauty (brought on by a symphony, a poem, or a work of art) that passed almost before he was aware of experiencing them. These moments were the joy that surprised him and led him to begin to think, "There's something more. There's something better than what I experience in the every day."

Theologians might describe all of these experiences as a hunger for shalom. If we know the word at all, we usually know it either as a Jewish greeting or as the Jewish word for peace. But shalom is much more than that. It is wholeness, rightness, things being just as they should be—life in communion (with God, with each other, and with all of creation). This is what we were made for. We have rarely, if ever, experienced it. For most of us, the closest we've come is a fleeting moment that is gone almost before we are aware of it. But this is what life was meant to be. This is what the Garden was like and what Jesus came to restore. This is the Great Banquet Jesus kept talking about over and over. This is big.

How did we lose it? How can we get it back? Those are two big questions that point to a very big story.

---

3. Lewis, *Surprised by Joy*, 72–78.

Lars and the Real Girl

ONE OF THE ODDEST and most interesting films of 2007 was *Lars and the Real Girl*, written by Nancy Oliver and directed by Craig Gillespie. Lars is a profoundly withdrawn man, long traumatized by death and dysfunction in his childhood. He lives in a rural community, on family property with his brother and sister-in-law, but essentially is unable to interact in any real way with others. Lars is around people, but he is utterly alone.

Early in the movie, Lars purchases a life-sized, inflatable female doll, created to be a sex toy. He has no intent of using the doll in that way, however. As his brother and sister-in-law quickly discover, Lars has the delusion that the doll is actually a real woman, Bianca, with whom he has been corresponding and who has come for a visit. Bianca is a missionary and, like Lars, values chastity. Lars asks if Bianca can stay in his brother's guest room and proceeds to interact with her as if they are having actual conversations. Lars's brother is horrified that Lars has, at last, completely given in to insanity, but the local physician suggests that the best way to help Lars is to interact with him and Bianca on Lars's terms.

While the members of Lars's church, the town folk, and, most of all, Lars's brother are initially incredulous, they go along. They all soon discover that Bianca has provided them with a door into Lars's life. He begins to form relationships with members of the community for the first time as they interact with him and Bianca. Over time, the town folk suggest that perhaps Bianca would like to get out on her own, and they invite her to read to children at the hospital (through a tape recorder), model clothes at the local dress shop (she does stand still wonderfully well), and eventually run for the school board (she wins the election). As all of this happens, as members of the town reach out to Lars by interacting with Bianca as if she were real, Lars begins to heal. He begins to be able to form relationships with others even when Bianca is not present.

In a very real sense, God's interaction with humanity is not unlike the people of Lars's community interacting with him. God is transcendent. God is *Other* than us—beyond our ability to comprehend. Relationships with others were beyond Lars's ability. He could not connect. Early in the movie, his brother laments Lars's inability to be normal and tries to get him to sit down to even one simple dinner, but to no avail. Lars cannot adapt to the ways of normal human interaction. He is in too much pain. He is too broken.

So the town adapts to Lars. He cannot enter their world, so they enter his. They step into the "relationship" he has with Bianca, and in doing so, are able to begin to relate to Lars. This is a bit of what the incarnation is like. The Gospel of Matthew says Jesus was *Emmanuel*, a word that means "God with us."

Creation itself is an incarnating act, an act of God coming to us. Christian theology maintains that God existed before all that we know as creation, or the physical world, came into being. It also maintains that God was complete in this prior existence. By that, it means that God didn't need for there to be an Earth, the galaxies that make up the universe, you, or me. And yet, God *desires* to create. And God desires to create beings who *can know and experience* Him.

Try thinking about it this way. When you speak, or write a poem, or paint a picture, you are expressing yourself. You are taking something that is within you—a thought, idea, or emotion—and putting it out there, communicating it to others. It is an expression of yourself. Self-expression is an act that seeks, on some level, to be understood by and connected with another. Creation, in a similar way, is God's self-expression but with an important distinction. If God is truly transcendent, unfathomably more than us, God could self-express and we would be utterly unable to understand, to comprehend. That creation is knowable to our senses, that we can feel anything of love at all, speaks to the idea that God conforms God's self-expression to fit us. Lars needed the townspeople to talk to him through Bianca, and so they did. We need God to "incarnate" in ways that we can comprehend, so God does.

God isn't just the beauty of a sunset, or the kindness of a friend's embrace, or even the wisdom of Jesus' teaching, but all of those things are vehicles or conduits through which God reveals God's self to us. C. S. Lewis used the following analogy to describe the same thing.[1] He suggested that we imagine a being that lived in the two-dimensional world of a postcard. That world would seem very real to him and would be all that he could conceive. Imagine then that word came to this being that there was a three dimensional world, a world that wasn't flat but that had

---

1. Lewis, "Transposition," 101.

texture and depth. The only way to communicate this would be to somehow find terms and concepts that were understandable to a "flatlander." Any two-dimensional description of the three dimensional world would always be incomplete. It could never be the real 3D reality, expressed in a 2D world, but it would *point to it*. In a similar way, God is not limited to or fully contained in the ways we experience God (be they nature, the Bible, stirrings in our heart, or stories of Jesus), but those can all be truthful doorways through which God can enter our 2D universe and be known.

In quirky and bizarre yet beautiful ways, the people around Lars enter into his world through the inflatable doll, Bianca. God enters our world through what we can experience and fathom. God does so first through creation itself and, later, through *Emmanuel,* Jesus.

Let *Us* Make Them Like *Us*

WHY ARE MADE FOR relationships? Why are we only ourselves when we are in proper relationship with others? Why do we ache for a sense of shalom, a state where all are in communion or relationship and all is well? Because we reflect *the Other* who made us.

One of the more complex doctrines of Christianity is that somehow God is One and also, at the same time, Three. This is the doctrine of the Trinity. For a good part of my life, I viewed the idea of the Trinity as a doctrine, an idea that one needed to believe in, maybe try to understand, and then file away in some dust-encased cabinet as one got on with real life. Over the last few years, I've come to view the Trinity very differently. I think the Trinity might be, at the risk of sounding like the 1990s TV show *The X-Files*, the *secret of everything*.

The doctrine of the Trinity argues that somehow God is One God, and within that God are three beings who are their own distinct persons, and yet who are also seamlessly and always relationally connected to one another—Father, Son, and Holy Spirit.

At times, people have tried to describe this as One God having three functions—the Father being that part of God that creates and orders all things, the Son being that part of God who comes to us and dies for us, and the Holy Spirit being God as movement, the part of God that indwells us and changes us. That view of the Trinity is helpful to a degree, but it fails quite significantly. It doesn't give us any sense of there actually being three persons or any sense of the unique relationship between them. We just have one God and three different roles.

Others have described the Trinity as being like water. At times it is liquid, at times ice, and at other times steam. God is one substance, but three states. Again, however, where's the relationship?

Of course, part of the problem here is the issue of idols and icons that we discussed earlier. In trying to come up with human terms or images that fit our human understanding of the physical world, we are trying to fit a three-dimensional reality into a two-dimensional world. Still, can we get closer? The images I am going to suggest are far from perfect, but perhaps each might contribute some piece of what is happening here, and together they might point to the whole.

The relational Trinity means that, somehow, there exists within God three distinct personalities who are yet thoroughly interrelated and interdependent. Also (and this is, I will admit, one of the most mind-bending ideas), while each is its own being, it also shares the same essence as the other two. In other words, the Father is not "more God" than the Son. There's nothing in the Father that is not in the Son or the Holy Spirit. The Son would not ever act in a way unlike how the Father and Spirit would act as well. In a very real sense, it is the interrelatedness, the *relationality among* the Father-Son-Holy Ghost that *is* God.

Perhaps thinking of an atom will help. Protons, neutrons, and electrons are each distinct, but they are also interrelated. If any of the three were missing, the others could not exist without it. Protons must find balance with electrons. This gets at the interdependence but doesn't get at the shared essence of the Trinity. The different parts of the atom are interdependent but fundamentally different from one another.

Mothers and children provide helpful images. In the womb, the infant forms and grows. It is a being and yet it is fully dependent upon the mother for life. In fact, for quite a while the line between mother and child is blurred. The state of the child in the womb affects the mother and vice versa. The two are different and yet one. This is not a perfect picture because the mother and the in utero child are clearly not equally dependent, but the image helps, perhaps.

Even after birth, this connection or relationship can continue. Elizabeth nursed both of our daughters for the first year of their lives. One of her favorite memories of that time would be the nights (which were most nights of the week) that the baby would wake up and Elizabeth would sleepily get up, take her to the couch, and lie with her, both half asleep while the baby nursed. Elizabeth describes feeling the child's heartbeat and breathing, the baby relaxing to the calm heartbeat of her mother, and the tiny mouth nursing at its mother's breast. Elizabeth will say there are few, if any, moments in her life where she has felt as at one with another being or as closely connected relationally.

Human embrace provides another image. In an embrace, I am holding and being held. I am opening myself to another and being received at the same time. I remain a distinct being, taking up a distinct space, but, at the same time, I am sharing a space with another, creating a reality that cannot exist without me or the other.

Or consider a surgeon's instrument. It is not the surgeon's hand, or mind, or nerve endings, but as it enters the patient's body, in a real sense the instrument is an extension of the surgeon. Through the instrument, the surgeon acts on the patient, and through the instrument she, in turn, experiences and senses the patient. The instrument is not the surgeon, per se, but in a sense, it *is* her. All it does is an extension of the hand that holds it.[1]

What is impossible to convey in these images, of course, is the equality and unity of essence in the Trinity. A mother and daughter may share a great deal, but they are not equal beings. The mother is in control in almost every sense. The instrument in the surgeon's hand, an extension of the surgeon though it may be, is, in the end, merely an inanimate tool.

One summer while working at a Young Life camp when I was in college, several other college kids and I engaged for a couple weeks in "the serving game." We had been reading Bible verses about the value of serving others and began to jokingly compete at serving one another. "Let me take those dishes back to the kitchen for you." That was a nice serve, but might it be a double serve to serve you by allowing you to serve me? By letting you carry my burden and so allowing you to gain service points, might I actually be amassing points for myself? It was a silly game, obviously. But, in a sense, it captures a Trinitarian reality. Part of the nature of the Trinity is a sense of three beings constantly deferring to each other, serving the others without ever becoming subservient. Our game at camp included this concept: "I don't ever need to worry about my rights or guard against being taken advantage of because I know you will take those precautions for me."

Here's another way of looking at it. I go out and act, and you watch me. You think, "That's *exactly* what I would have done. The way you responded to that was perfectly in tune with how I would have responded." Except, in the case of the Trinity, while the Son might be in the world acting, the Father and Holy Spirit are present, not watching from a distance.

Jesus (any surprise?) provides an even better image. In the Gospel of John, mere hours before his death, he seeks to comfort his closest friends. He describes how he and God his Father are one, and he tells his friends that they can participate in that relationship of oneness as well. He describes this with an image from nature: "I am the vine, you are the

---

1. I owe this illustration to the scientist and philosopher Michael Polanyi, *Personal Knowledge*, 58–59.

branches." A vine with the branches growing from it and the fruit growing from the branches expresses this relationality. All are different and yet all are part of the same plant.

First John says that God is love. This is quite a bit different than saying, "God is tall" or "God is skinny." Love is a verb. To be a verb, one must act. Love is so many things: giving, receiving, caring, relating. Unless God became love when our world was created (God now having something or someone to love), God has always related, always loved. Again, this is who God is.

All that is to say this: We are beings that are only truly ourselves when we relate, because that is who God is. Genesis tells us that we are made in the image of God. We are the *imago dei*. It can be tempting to think of this individually, that God looks like me, with hair, a face, two arms. This is a mistake. Genesis states it this way: "Let *us* create God in *our* image . . . In the image of God he created *them. Male and female he created them.*" When are we God's image? When we are in relationship with one another and with God. This is so because this is who God is.

Relational Selves

L ET ME EXPAND ON this idea of humans being made for relationships
with an illustration from science. In the 1960s, Harry Harlow conducted experiments on baby rhesus monkeys. To varying degrees, he de-
prived infant monkeys of interaction with their mothers, other monkeys,
or human surrogates. The results were striking and controversial. His
experiments determined that, even when all other needs were provided,
an absence of interaction with others profoundly scarred the monkeys.
So much so that his experiments are often considered key to the rise of
the animal rights movement. Meeting all of the monkeys' needs *except*
interaction with others caused many to accuse Harlow of torture and to
view him as a monster.

We humans shouldn't be so shocked. Short of the death penalty or
physical torture, what is the most severe form of punishment in our penal
system? Solitary confinement. We punish people by denying them human
interaction. It is easier to go prolonged periods of time without creature
comforts than it is to go without other people.

On a positive note but making the same point, one of the most effec-
tive ways to help seriously ill patients in hospitals is to give them a pet.
The same principle holds true for the elderly. People live longer when they
have a pet to care for and interact with. Why? How is it that a puppy can
have more effect than thousands of dollars in medical treatments?

We crave interaction and relationship, and when we don't have it,
we suffer. What is it about us that causes us to ache for others? How is it
that we can have everything we need for health, but if we are isolated and
alone, we will fail to thrive? If even infants display an awareness that they
need relational connections with others, what does this tell us about what
it means to be a person?

My hunch is that it tells us that being a person may be very intimately tied up with being in relationships. Relationships, friendship, and love
may not be just the icing on the cake, the things that make my self happy.
They may also be the very things that make me a self in the first place.

Over the last few centuries, and nowhere more than in America, we
have tended to glorify the individual. Who are American heroes? Our
heroes are rugged individuals, those who "go it alone." They are cowboys

sitting atop their horses, riding alone into the sunset, needing no one, fully self-sustaining and self-contained.

Perhaps the self-contained individual is a lie. Perhaps, after all, we truly *do* need others to be fully healthy, to fully "be ourselves." I would like to suggest something even further. Not only do we need others to fill out, top off, or round out our *selves*. We are also only truly *selves at all* when we are in relationships.

Many premodern civilizations seem to support this. In tribal and aboriginal cultures, anything that looks like Western individualism is absent. The borders of the self are permeable, and the others in the village and all of nature itself are included within the definition of *self*. In such civilizations, the self is not a closed, walled off system but one that is open and in dynamic relationship with others. In this sense, a self does not exist alone but only in relation with others. Throughout modernity in the West, it has been tempting to dismiss this view as pantheistic or animistic and superstitious. While that may be true, the West should not be so quick to dismiss all that is going on in these cultures. Animism is clearly not a Christian idea; I'm not proposing that we adopt it. *I am* proposing that the autonomous, self-contained self of the West is also not a Christian idea and that what is needed is an understanding of self that suggests our being both distinct and also connected and dependent upon the other.

We thrive when we are in relationship. We whither and suffer when we are isolated and alone. Even language suggests that we are selves only in relationship. The existence of language is rooted in our desire, our need, to communicate. We speak to be heard. We write words to have them read.

The philosopher Descartes famously grounded selfhood in the mind, saying, "I think, therefore I am." I am suggesting an alternative: "I relate, therefore I am." In the twentieth century, Jewish philosopher Martin Buber wrote a famous book entitled, *I and Thou*.[1] He argued that the interaction of a self with another is the central reality of our experience. Tragically, however, we have turned our potentially I-You interactions into I-It. What he meant was that we treat the Other as an It, a thing.

How can this be? Think about it for a moment. Have you ever had a coach who you felt saw you as "a winner" or "a loser" but not as a person? If you are a woman, have you ever interacted with a man who you felt "objectified" you sexually? Have you ever met someone and thought, "Oh,

---

1. Buber, *I and Thou*, 73–75.

he's a black (or a jock, or a liberal)," before you thought of him as a person? Have you ever been kind to teachers, peers, or family members to get something that you wanted and that they could give and not because of who they were? The possible examples could go on endlessly. All of this is what Buber would call turning the fundamental You into an It.

It doesn't end there, however. He further argues that in turning You into an It, we are "de-selfed" as well. It's as if you took the title, *I and Thou*, and rooted selfhood in the *and* of that phrase. Perhaps the monkeys that had needed relationships to thrive or the patients who get better when they have a pet are just more accurately reflecting a reality most of us are able to hide a good bit of the time. We are never whole unless we are relationally whole.

Naked and Not Ashamed, for a While

DEBATES HAVE RAGED FOR centuries about whether Adam and Eve are historical figures who literally talked to a snake and ate a piece of fruit from a specific tree or whether they are mythological figures meant to communicate an idea. I am not going to wade into that debate. I do think that whether historical fact or mythological legend, their story accurately describes a great deal of what was once wonderfully right with all of us and has gone wrong. Let's slow down and take a closer look.

One of the interesting things about the way the first couple of chapters of Genesis describe life in the Garden comes in the last sentence of the story: "The man and his wife were both naked, *and they felt no shame.*" No embarrassment. No, "Hey, why did you look at me like that?" No comparing. No thoughts of, "If only I were more this or less that." No thoughts of themselves, really, at all.

Life in Genesis was a life lived without barriers to relationship with each other or with God. No imperfections to hide. No motives to doubt. No reason to say one thing but really mean another. Just humans relating, unfiltered and unhindered with one another and with God. They were not objects of lust or comparison. They were simply beings in relationship.

Forget for a moment that very quickly the whole picture changed, for them and for us. For now, let's sit for a bit on what this was like.

A couple of years ago, I was asked by some students, as we were discussing the possibility or impossibility of modeling Jesus' level of engagement with the world while still maintaining purity, how the fully human Jesus was able to so immerse himself in tempting situations without ever sinning. An idea occurred to me that may shed some light on how the human side of Jesus is able to do this.

How do doctors and nurses spend all day working with people who have no clothes on without lusting after them? How is a hospital nothing like a strip club? I believe it is because when doctors or nurses are in the presence of that naked body, they don't see a pair of breasts or a great set of abs or anything like that. They see a person who needs them. They see a person with a problem and they see *only* that. Of course, this is not *always* the case, but you get the idea.

I think this is something like Jesus' experience and something like what Adam and Eve had in the Garden. Jesus didn't see scantily clad and seductively postured prostitutes. He saw women who were lonely and lost. He saw women who needed to be seen and cared for and loved, not as objects but as persons. I believe the same is true for Adam and Eve. They had no shame in their nakedness because they never conceived of themselves or one another in self-conscious ways. They related with one another and with God. Period.

This meant being present with and for another person. Being able to see and be seen without fear or judgment. Seeing only the Relation, not the other or myself, as object. To not hide, withhold, or guard from one another. These are things that we can scarcely conceive because they are so alien to our existence. We primarily know insecurity, fear, hiding, objectifying, and judging.

We know these things in our relationships with each other, and we know them in relation to God. In walking through the Garden, like friends out on an evening stroll around the block, Adam and Eve are experiencing an intimacy with God that is foreign to us. There is no distance to be bridged, no mediation required. There's just God and humans, out for an evening walk. People argue about whether there was a literal Garden at all and whether an actual Adam and Eve experienced this or the events that follow. I believe there was, but I also believe that if it is all just a myth, it is a profoundly insightful one. It speaks of what we ache to experience and what we tragically have lost.

In a strange way, however, this story is also hopeful. There is hope because this story says, "This is not the natural order of things. This is not what life was made to be like." The Church throughout history has spent a lot of time talking about Original Sin, or the idea that we all are broken, but if that idea is true, doesn't it suggest that there was something before? Some time when we weren't broken and, maybe, if that is true, we could be put back together again?

PART TWO

Where Did Things Go So Horribly Wrong?

*L*ET'S BE HONEST: THE *world of shalom, of open, free relationships of trust and love with God and one another, doesn't look much at all like what we experience in our day-to-day lives. What happened? The Bible tells a vivid story of how humanity ended up here and what God does about it. Our experience, or at least mine, seems to confirm almost all of the Bible's perspective.*

One way of framing this discussion would be to see it as a look at the concept of "sin" and how that plays itself out in individual lives and in the world. Sin can be a loaded term for some of us. Perhaps it's been thrown at you accusatorily ("You are a sinner!"), or perhaps it just sounds archaic and distant. To a large extent, I don't think using the word sin really matters that much. We could completely avoid the term and still honestly face the reality that people often do, that I often do, horrible things to one another. Most of us would agree that we have a sense that selfless concern for others, kindness, humility, and so on, would be the best way to live, and yet, we also would agree that we have a very difficult, if not impossible, time living that way. Many of us resonate with the idea that we were meant, as discussed in Part One, to have a harmonious, relational connection to God, and yet we often feel a deep alienation instead.

Why is this?

The Three by Meghan Hedley

Life and Death on the Playground

DANNY SCHWARTZ SAT IN front of me for two years in fourth and fifth grade. *Schwartz, Sherwood:* Our names were in alphabetical order on the seating chart. Danny, in the tiny and yet all-encompassing world of my elementary school class, was easily the least popular kid. For one thing, he was way smarter than everyone else. While the rest of us were reading at a basic level and mostly watching a lot of television, Danny was reading J. R. R. Tolkien's *The Lord of the Rings*. Mostly though, Danny was very nervous. And when he got nervous, he scratched the back of his neck and rocked back and forth. He didn't scratch his neck in a subtle, unnoticeable way. He scratched it like he was going to dig the skin right off. He rocked forward and back as if he were in a rocking chair. Danny was nervous a lot of the time. Kids being kids, most everyone responded to that by making fun of Danny, pretty much all the time.

In a way that I desperately tried to hide from everyone in the class, I had become Danny's friend. Because we sat next to each other for two years in a row, we often worked on projects together. I got better grades when I worked with Danny. I wasn't reading *The Lord of the Rings,* but my Dad was a big fan and was reading them to my brother and me at night, which was sort of the same thing. We weren't sleepover kind of friends, but the truth was that doing projects with and talking to Danny could really be interesting and fun.

I don't remember what I'd been doing that day at recess—probably playing four-square. That's what I did most every day at recess. What I do remember is walking around the corner and seeing Danny. Actually, I remember seeing Danny and almost all the boys in my class. As usual, everybody was taunting him. The topic varied from day to day: his clothes, his glasses, his scratching his neck, his being a "brainiac." What remained relentlessly unvaried was him being teased about *something*. Today's topic was Danny's lack of friends.

"You don't have any friends, Danny! No one likes you."

Danny responded as he did every day: by cowering, rocking, and feverishly scratching his neck—somehow trying to survive the daily hell that was fifth grade for him.

And then he saw me come around the corner.

Uncharacteristically, Danny stopped rocking, stopped scratching, and straightened up. Confidently he said, "Yes I do! Steve is my friend." He pointed at me. Nobody had seen me walk up. I wasn't on the bottom of the pile like Danny, but I was hardly the Big Man on Campus either. Now everyone turned to me.

It literally took me about two seconds to figure out what was going on and even less time for me to decide what I was going to do. Actually, to say I decided implies that I weighed various options. I don't remember doing that. I remember responding reflexively, as if the choice was so obvious that it didn't even require thought.

With everyone turned to me and Danny looking at me with a semi-confident, semi-pleading smile, I knew exactly what to say.

"No you don't, Danny. You don't have any friends. I'm not your friend."

The crowd of boys erupted with joy. All eyes returned to Danny.

"Told you!"

"Hah! Not even Sherwood likes you."

I felt horrible for Danny. I watched hope drain from his face and despair settle in. Mostly though, I felt relief. The eyes, *the eye*, was off of me. It had worked. I'd been spared.

In the two seconds it took to appraise the situation, I knew what claiming Danny as a friend would do for him. It would save his life. It would save him in that moment and for as long as he was in that school. He would no longer be alone, no longer alone to face ridicule. Adrift in the shark-infested ocean of Schuylkill Elementary School, he'd have a friend. He'd have some small scrap of community.

What I knew even more powerfully, however, was what it would mean for me. Giving Danny that gift would cost me. He'd no longer be alone because I would join him. It was him or me. No debate; it wasn't even close.

I apologized to Danny later. He said it was okay, that he understood. More than anyone, he probably did. It didn't matter, though. I knew who I was. I knew what I had done. I'd always felt proud that I'd not joined the harshest taunting of Danny. Sure, when he wasn't around, I might scratch my neck and rock to get a laugh, to show that I belonged. But I didn't do it to his face like everyone else. I was different. I was better.

As it turned out, I wasn't better at all. If anything, I might have been worse. Everyone else was being cruel to someone they didn't really know, someone they didn't even see as a person, another kid. I knew Danny. Not in a way that included doing things together outside of school, but in as real a way as Danny had, I was his friend. I knew that. It even made me feel kind of good about myself. It made me feel morally superior.

Until it looked like it would cost me something.

What the Bible calls sin is a complicated and multifaceted thing. At the same time, it is a stunningly simple thing. Sin is this moment on the fifth-grade playground. Faced with a choice, I chose me. I always did. I always do. On a very basic level, this is what sin is.

At the center of my universe is me—first, last, and always. I have moments where this doesn't appear so. There are moments where I am kind to others, where I give to charities, where I offer a helping hand. Even in these moments, though, *me* is still front and center. I'm brilliant at quickly and subtly calculating the math. What is the advantage *to me* of this act of kindness? Will I be thought well of? Will this person love me back? Will the benefit of that outweigh the cost? If so, I'm in. Look at me. Great guy. If not, well, maybe some other time.

In the early twentieth century, the *London Times* hosted an essay contest, "What's wrong with the world?" This contest was hosted during the height of the Modern Era. It was a time when humanity, at least humanity in "civilized" places like Europe and the United States, was brimming with confidence that we had everything we needed to right all that was wrong in the world. The only question was to figure out which problem to conquer first. Hence, the contest.

All kinds of literary, philosophical, political, and religious heavyweights were invited to write essays for the paper, weighing in with their thoughts about what humanity's most significant (but surely soon to be eradicated) problem was. One of those was the Catholic writer G. K. Chesterton. He wrote a strikingly short essay in response. His response was only two words, in fact.

What's wrong with the world? "I am."

No one who knew or read Chesterton would have taken this response as evidence of poor self-esteem. That was not the issue. What Chesterton meant was that most all of our massive societal issues—war, injustice, violence, and on and on—have a very clear individual component to them. Take my behavior on the Schuylkill School playground. Play it out through my lifetime of self-serving, self-protecting choices. Multiply this by the few billion people alive at this moment. Multiply that again by all the people who have ever lived. Is it any surprise that the world seems like a profoundly screwed up place?

The endless optimism of the Modern Era turned out to be a lie. It didn't bring the end of all that ails humanity. It ended up in the gas chambers of Auschwitz. Something is terribly wrong. Something is terribly wrong with me. Something is terribly wrong with us.

About the same time that the scene with Danny took place, my family was watching a series on PBS called *The World at War*, which was a documentary series on World War II. The episodes that dealt with the Holocaust were devastating. As a grade school kid, how does one make sense of that? How could people do that? How I made sense of it is how most of us, kids or otherwise, do. *They* did that. *People like that* are capable of *those kinds of things. People like us* never could do that.

At the same time, my parents had bought a recently published book called *Bury My Heart at Wounded Knee* by Dee Brown. It told the history of what we would now call the First Nations, or Native Americans, and their interactions with first European and then American culture. It was not the story that I'd seen on TV movies growing up in the late 1960s and early 1970s. It was not the story of brave settlers fighting off savages. It was the story of genocide and broken promises. It did great damage to my view that *those kinds of people (Nazis) do those kinds of things, but we would never do that.* My ancestors had in fact done deeds almost as horrible as those done by the Nazis.

That's really the point of my story about Danny. I didn't devastate a continent of civilizations or send six million Jews to the ovens, but in a real sense, I clearly chose Danny's "death" that day over my own. Most of the Germans weren't any different from me. Neither were the Europeans and early generations of Americans who all but wiped out Native American civilization on this continent. I am just like them. The only difference was one of scale.

> *"I suspect that most people don't need Satan to recruit them to evil. They are quite capable of recruiting themselves."*[1]
> —M. Scott Peck

1. Peck, *People of the Lie*, 38.

Evanescence

THAT WE OFTEN FEEL alone and ache not to be so is not a new idea. I can remember when the collective weight of it crashed down on me, however. I was working at a Young Life camp in the summer of 2003 when a particularly hardened group of kids from Colorado arrived in camp. Watching them get off the bus, it was obvious that this group of kids would be different than most. In the ninety-degree weather, most of them wore full-length trench coats. None of them had hair that was its original color, and they all had some quantity of black makeup. The more sedate just had black lipstick, but others had black teardrops drawn on their cheeks or half of their faces covered in a painted-on mask.

As the week got under way, it was clear that the clothes and makeup were not just a temporary display. During the first twenty-four hours of the week, the dozen or so young people in this group refused to participate in anything going on in the camp of more than three hundred kids. A good bit of the time they would sit in the back, facing away from whatever was going on up front.

Bob and J. J., the two men in charge of the "program" of the week, were desperate to figure out a way to connect on even a small level with these kids. At Young Life camps, the evening meetings begin with a half-hour or so of singing. Though a Young Life camp is a place to share the Gospel, most of the singing is not explicitly "Christian," and much of it is music that young people would be familiar with from the radio. Bob and J. J. decided that perhaps music might provide a door to connect with these teens. They sat down with the adult leaders who'd brought the group and asked, "What do your kids like musically? Is there anything they like that we'd be able to play?"

The group's leaders suggested a song that Bob and J. J. had never heard of, but the two decided to learn it and spent all of that afternoon practicing the song. While they had hopes that this small group of Goth kids would somehow appreciate the effort, they were sure that for the other three hundred, the song would be a disaster. The song was dark. It wasn't (at least not at this point) a top-forty, or even top-one-hundred, hit, and it involved several sections where two voices would yell lyrics back and forth to each other. Practicing that afternoon, Bob and J. J. both thought it was going to be an awkward and unsuccessful three to four minutes trying to lead this song.

After starting out with the more typical fare (a little "Brown Eyed Girl" or boy band stuff), they introduced the song they'd learned for the Goth kids. "Hey, we're guessing this is a new song to most of you, but if you know it, jump in with us."

Within seconds, it was clear that they had underestimated the three hundred kids sitting in the room and the power of the song. Sitting in the back of the room, I first had goose bumps run over my body and then tears well up in my eyes. I've been at more than twenty years of Young Life camps, and I'd never heard a room full of kids sing a song with the level of intensity that they sang this song. While they enjoyed singing most of what Bob and J. J. led, they sang this song like it rose from the core of their very being.

The song was "Bring Me to Life" by Evanescence, and it later became massively popular, eventually winning a Grammy Award. It swells, line after line, until it literally screams about emptiness, isolation, and feeling barely alive. While a room of a few hundred kids might sing an old Beatles tune or something by Justin Timberlake with a fair bit of enthusiasm, I'd *never* heard anything like this room, singing that song.

It was as if, for a moment, this mass of more than three hundred adolescents decided to say, "You want to know who we are? You want to get a peek at what our lives *really* look like, feel like? Well, here it is." It was overwhelming. Afterward, any adult in the room that I talked to echoed the same sentiments: "What was that?! I knew kids were hurting, but I had no idea!"

Those four minutes set the stage for a remarkable week, and not just with that group of Goth kids from Colorado. Across the board, having had the curtain pulled back a bit, adults and the adolescents they had brought had conversations throughout the week at a depth few of us ever had encountered before.

What was going on there? At the risk of taking a profound experience and reducing it to the absurd, the best metaphor to describe it, in my mind, comes from a children's story. In "The Emperor's New Clothes," two crooks deceive the Emperor into thinking they have sold him an outfit of such dazzling beauty that only the wisest can even see it. In reality, they have sold him air. He puts on his new outfit and parades through the streets of the city. For quite a while, everyone (including the Emperor himself), through fear of being labeled "fools" who cannot see, pretend that the Emperor is, in fact, wearing a stunningly beautiful suit of clothes. Finally, a small child blurts out the obvious—"The emperor is wearing no clothes!"—and the charade falls apart.

I think this is illustrative of how we move through our days. How many of us have been greeted on the street by a friend who asks, "Hey, how are you doing?" to which we reply, "Great," when the exact opposite was the truth? The Modern Era told us that we were self-contained, self-sufficient. It led us to believe that we didn't need anyone. By and large, we live our lives acting like that's really true and that we're all "great." Those three hundred kids in a room in Minnesota were singing a truth that is really true for virtually all of us. The Emperor really does have no clothes. As the song's lyrics suggested, the faces that we put forward of being "fine" and "doing great" are often lies; an emptiness is inside.

Thoughts from Others on Human Isolation

"The slow sure doom falls, pitiless and dark." [1]
—Bertrand Russell

"Most men live lives of quiet desperation." [2]
—Henry David Thoreau

*"Most men and women lead lives at the worst so painful, at the best so
monotonous, the desire for escape, the longing to transcend themselves if
only for a few moments is and always has been,
one of the principle appetites of the soul."* [3]
—Aldous Huxley

*"The most terrible poverty is loneliness, and the feeling
of being unloved."* [4]
—Mother Teresa of Calcutta

"It is strange to be so known so universally and yet be so lonely." [5]
—Albert Einstein

1. Russell, *Mysticism and Logic*, 40.

2. Thoreau, *Walden*, 6.

3. Huxley, quoted by Dallas Willard, *Divine Conspiracy*, 83.

4. Mother Teresa, quoted on thinkexist.com.

5. Einstein, quoted on thinkexist.com.

The Year the Pain Wouldn't Stop

FOR ME, 1992 WAS an awful year. It began with the death of a high school student, Al Hart, who was involved with me in Young Life, from complications related to pneumonia. It ended with two of my cousins, both in high school, dying from a car crash while driving home from school. The events in between seemed, if anything, almost worse.

At Frontier Ranch, Young Life's camp in Buena Vista, Colorado, one of the guys in my cabin seemed exceedingly upset as the week drew to a close. After a couple of hours sitting with him, he shared that he was sure that he was a pedophile. A little stunned by this, I asked him what in the world made him think that. I reassured him that I, and everyone who knew him, found him to be loving and caring. It was at this point that he shared that he'd been sexually abused for an extended time by a family friend and church leader.

Abuse became the theme of that summer. A close friend, a peer in ministry, shared that she had been sexually victimized in college by a man also in Christian ministry. Efforts to have him removed from ministry were largely met with defensiveness and denials. My friend, at this point, had already been in a few years of counseling.

At the end of the summer, I was at a meeting with ministry peers. There we were informed that the leader of the group had been forced to leave ministry due to sexually inappropriate behavior with a high school student. We were stunned. At the meeting, someone asked how the abuse was discovered. We were told that the abuser had been a part of a team of adults working at a summer camp where the sexual misconduct had occurred. One of the women on the staff there for the month had recognized the signs in his behavior because she had had the same experiences with him more than a decade earlier.

I sat at that meeting trying to figure out whom in the world they could be talking about. I knew another close friend of mine (in fact, a woman I had dated) had been on that team. Perhaps I should call her and find out. As I thought about it, I thought more about my friend's story. She had grown up in the community where this man did ministry. She had been intimately involved in the local ministry there, starting as a high school student and extending well beyond high school. He spoke nationally about that ministry and often described her in almost saint-like terms.

As I sat in this room of fifty people and the conversation moved on to other implications of this man's leaving ministry, it all became clear to me. I didn't need to call her to find out what was going on. I knew what was going on. *She* was the one who turned him in. She was the one who had recognized what he was doing because he had done it to her. The woman I had dated had been the victim of the man who over and over spoke of her glowingly to others.

I apologize for the description I'm about to use, but for a long time, I described those months as the "year spent up to my neck in shit." Everywhere I turned, it seemed the reality I encountered was that of people I loved being horrifically wounded by those they should have been able to trust. People who should have protected and nurtured them had instead brutalized them.

In the last chapter, I talked about "sin" in terms of myself and in ways that suggested that all of us are culpable in contributing to the world's brokenness. I believe that to be true. We all are sinners. We all choose to think of self before God or others, and the results are disastrous and permanent. Apart from God providing a means of grace for us, we are hopelessly lost.

We covered that ground in the previous chapter, and if I wanted to continue on that theme, I could easily talk more about the three men who victimized my loved ones. I'd rather, at this point, talk about the ones I loved. The Bible talks about sin in profound ways. One, as we've noted, is about our personal responsibility for sin. The other is in terms of sin from which we need to be rescued, sin from which we need deliverance.

In Genesis, the offspring of Abraham end up as invited guests in Egypt. For a time, they prosper there and are welcomed. After a few generations, however, they prove to be so prosperous that they become a threat to Egyptian power. The beginning of the book of Exodus tells this part of the story. Threatened by the Israelites, the pharaoh of Egypt enslaves them. He puts them to work, ruthlessly forcing them to build the great cities of Egypt. When the Israelites continue to thrive, he resorts to genocide. All Jewish male infants were to be drowned at birth.

God sees what is going on and is moved. The writer of the story tells it like this: "I [God speaking to Moses] have seen the misery of my people who are in Egypt; I have heard them crying out on account of their slave drivers, and I am concerned about their sufferings. So I have come down to rescue them ..."

Prior to the Exodus (God's use of Moses to deliver the Israelites from slavery in Egypt), the Israelites had really been just a very large family clan. The Exodus and the events that followed (receiving the Ten Commandments and the rest of the Law on Mount Sinai) constitute the founding story of the nation of Israel. Every nation has its "founding fathers and mothers" story. In America, we cherish our story of brave men and women who, against all odds and in the name of liberty, threw off the oppressive British and built a nation based upon freedom and justice. Our ancestors are heroes in our story, taking matters into their own hands.

Israel's founders are slaves. They are hopeless until God hears their cry and acts on their behalf. What does this have to do with sin? Just this: As important as it is to recognize our personal responsibility and guilt in sin, there is also a narrative in scripture of humanity being the *victims* of sin. The Exodus story is just one example in scripture. The Bible is constantly calling attention to the abuse and neglect of the poor and helpless. The Israelites in Egypt, children from abusive homes, and enslaved and oppressed peoples anywhere are victims of sin. In very real ways, we all are both guilty parties *and* wounded parties.

Christians can tend to see one reality and not the other. Some Christians talk about Jesus and the cross solely in terms of the cross dealing with our guilt before God. In fact, in these presentations, before getting to the great news of the cross, a lot of time is given to hammering home individual guilt due to sin.

Other Christians go in the other direction. These focus almost exclusively upon liberation—from economic injustice, racial inequity, sexism, or any power that oppresses. In this interpretation, God does not come to forgive; God comes to kick butt and take names! The Exodus story was a great source of comfort and identification to slaves in the American South, for instance, and to victims of injustice around the world.

Which is correct: Those who tout Jesus, the forgiver of the guilty, or those who champion Jesus, the liberator of the oppressed? How about both? Jesus is both the one who washes the guilty clean *and* the one who sets the captives free. Evangelicals (usually the personal-guilt orientated folks) could stand to bring in a good deal more of Jesus the Liberator. (In theological circles, this Jesus is sometimes described as *Christus Victor* (Christ the Victor) and the idea as a whole as Liberation Theology.)

Likewise, champions of the oppressed would be well served to recognize that even oppressed people are fallen and sinful in their own ways.

The Bible contains stories that emphasize individual guilt *and* stories that stress the need for deliverance from the sin of others. To me, this indicates that, as we talk about the work of Jesus on the cross, it is appropriate to talk of both, or to emphasize the story that our given audience most needs at the time. To the young man in my cabin, so devastated by the pain of his own abuse that he was sure he was doomed to abuse as well, did not need at that point to have me drive home his guilt before God. He needed hope that Jesus could bring deliverance. Once the truth of that message took hold, there would be a time for wrestling with individual guilt, but not right then. Likewise, I believe there are others who do need to hear, up front, the message of our individual culpability in sin.

Sin ravages. We hurt. We hurt at the hands of others, and we inflict hurt upon others. God, through the incarnating and sacrificial acts of Jesus, addresses both of these realities. Jesus is a healing balm, a mighty deliverer, and one who can wash us white as snow. He never performs just one of these functions. He performs *all* of them.

Two Moments Observed

IN THE TOWN WHERE I live, the high school and middle schools start class at 7:20 a.m. I often go for runs between six and seven o'clock in the morning, so I often see kids on their way to school. Here are two things I've seen.

A couple of years ago I ran through the parking lot and by the front of the middle school a mile from our home. It was 6:30 in the morning. One or two cars were in the lot, but it was well before most teachers and students arrived. As I ran by the cafeteria, with its solid wall of windows, I saw a twelve-to-thirteen-year-old boy sitting at a table. He wasn't reading, or doing homework, or texting on his cell phone. He was just sitting, staring at the wall in front of him.

Across the other side of the vast cafeteria, I saw another boy doing the same thing. Two boys. Obviously dropped off early because their folks had to get to work or something. Both of them were alone in the school, except for one another, and were sitting dozens of feet apart. Not talking. Not doing anything. Only staring.

The second scene happened just a few months ago. I was jogging down a hill in our neighborhood, and to my left was a beautiful sunrise—orange sky, with just enough clouds to provide stunning contrast to the deep blue above. As I approached the bottom of the hill and continued to be awed by the sky off to my left, I came upon a bus stop at which three high-school-aged kids, two boys and a girl, were waiting for the bus. Their backs were turned to the sunrise. They each stood at least eight to ten feet from the other. Each was silent. Each just stared at the ground, missing the beauty of the morning.

We often feel so alone. What comfort could we draw from the average people around us, if we'd only cross the room and start to talk?

"Man, it sucks to be here so early every day."

"It sure does."

As surely as those three kids at the bus stop had turned their backs upon and completely missed the beautiful sunrise, they were also turned from and closed to one another. What might God be trying to give us in the beauty of an orange sky and the company of others to share it with that we miss as our backs are turned, as we stare ahead in isolation?

Love, with a Price Tag

WE LEARN EARLY THAT, as a rule, love isn't cheap. It certainly does not come for free. One would hope that there'd be at least a few years of childhood where this wasn't the case, but I don't think there is. A family dinner at the Sherwood house a few years ago illustrates this.

At the time, our daughters, Bailey and Rachel, were four and two years old. Elizabeth and I love them profoundly. I cannot begin to tell you the joy they bring to my life. We eat meals together at least five nights a week. We read together, we wrestle on the floor, or we play in the backyard. If there are kids who would know that love should be free, it's my girls. Or so I had hoped.

Neither of the girls are what you'd call enthusiastic eaters. At least they were not in terms of that evening's prepared meal. Over the years, we've learned the five or six entrées they'll enthusiastically eat, and we pretty much stick to those. Sometimes, not even those work.

This was one of those evenings. Rachel, our two year old, was enthusiastically singing, getting up to go to the bathroom (for the third time), and moving food around her plate to form works of art. She was doing anything but putting food in her mouth and swallowing. This was nothing new. One or both of the girls were just as likely as not to act this way, so it wasn't all that stressful for Elizabeth and me. We were doing what we usually do: regularly reminding, cajoling, and nudging Rachel to eat, but not scolding or griping at her.

Bailey watched all this for a while and then chimed in with words I will never forget.

"Dad. I'm going to eat every bite of my dinner."

"Great, sweetie."

"You know why?"

"How come? Because you like it?"

"No! I'm going to eat every bite because *then you will love me.*"

Where the *heck* did that come from? How had this four year old, whose life to this point has been ninety percent comprised of interactions with Elizabeth and me, come to the conclusion that love was not a sure thing, that she needed to do something to get it? How had she come to the belief that love comes with a price tag?

I still don't have an answer for those questions. But I suspect it was because, one way or another, we *all* come to that conclusion. My Dad will love me if I am really good at football. My mom will love me if I sit up straight and don't scream in the grocery store. My coach will love me if I stay in the game, never mind the pain. My boss will love me if I put in a few extra hours. My wife will love me if I clean out those gutters.

The list of "he/she will love me if . . ." statements could go on forever. Two things are always true about the list. First, it's always personalized. Your list is different than mine. Bailey's is different than Rachel's. You can be sure that it's tailored just for you. The second thing is that it never ends. You could meet the demands of "you'll love me if . . ." for one hundred days in a row, but there will be something new on the list tomorrow.

Why should our sense of unworthiness, our sense of needing to perform to be loved, be so personalized? I cannot speak to all of the complexities of psychology and identity formation, but I have a couple ideas. Earlier we discussed the idea that, while we all share a great deal in common, we also uniquely reflect the image of God. I experience the world and God in ways that are unique and wonderfully specific to me. So do you. That being the case, is it then not surprising that the shattering of that experience would take on similarly unique forms? Whether we yearn to be viewed as popular, a great athlete, or the best student in class, the longing for some validation that will come from outside and complete us is true for us all.

We also move through our lives with stories that are uniquely ours. Even the child in a loving, supporting home has the one specific day where he or she breaks a glass and hears a parent chide, "How could you be so clumsy?!" Our wounds are our own. And they continue to fester and affect us far beyond what their initial bleeding would seem to indicate.

And why don't they stop? Why can't one grand gesture, or act, or word finally make them go away? For years I coached high school track. We had some very successful teams. At one point, I coached a young woman who desperately wanted to be the state three-thousand-meter champion and had the talent and drive to do it. Overcoming injuries that slowed her during her freshman year, she trained feverishly the winter and spring of her sophomore year and won the three-thousand on the first day of the three-day state meet. On the morning of the second day of the meet, I got up early and went down to the hotel lobby. To my surprise, she was already up and just sitting alone there in a chair.

I asked her what she was doing, and she replied, "Steve, I feel so awful! Since, junior high, I have been sure that if I were a state champion at something, I would finally feel good inside. I woke up this morning and I feel just the same. Still empty. Still not good enough."

I have a friend who spent several years as the team chaplain for the Washington Redskins of the NFL. During that time, the team won the Super Bowl, the pinnacle of achievement for a football player. Several members of the team expressed to him that the most depressing period of their lives were the days immediately following the Super Bowl triumph. They had literally spent years upon years of their lives sold out completely for the accomplishment of the goal of winning a Super Bowl. When they finally got there, they discovered that, as exciting and gratifying as the win was, it also left them strangely empty. They had pursued a dream that they thought would completely fulfill them, and when they got there, they struggled with the realization that it hadn't.

Have you ever tried to build a sandcastle at the ocean's edge? Not inland from the water but right where the waves play themselves out? No matter how much sand you add to your castle's outer wall, the water washes it away. No amount of effort can change the reality that the rushing water easily undoes your efforts. Perhaps, if you wanted to truly stop the tide, you'd need something other than sand. Perhaps, the hole inside of us that makes us feel so unworthy and inadequate can't be filled with more and better performance.

"(Too often) I am what I have, what I do, what people say about me." [1]
—Henri Nouwen

"You just want to be held and told you're worth it after all." [2]
—J. J. Alberhasky

---

1. Nouwen, quoted by Job and Shawchuck, *A Guide to Prayer*, 75.
2. Alberhasky, "Good Advice."

The Nought

Walker Percy was a Roman Catholic writer from the South who wrote about life in America in the last half of the twentieth century. He was a man who had experienced profound sadness. Several of his family members, including his father, grandfather, and perhaps his mother, committed suicide. He converted to Catholicism as an adult and there found the hope and meaning that he felt his family members, and Western society, lacked.

In two nonfiction books, *A Message in a Bottle*[1] and *Lost in the Cosmos*,[2] Percy discusses what it is like to live in the materialistic, scientific West. One of his primary ideas is the "noughted-self" ("nought" being another way of expressing the idea of "zero"). He describes the "noughted-self" something like this:

Picture the desire for a new set of clothes, a new iPod, a new car, or a new "look"—the kind of longing that most of us have experienced from time to time. Or picture the junior high kid (or forty-five year old!) who most days wears clothes representing his favorite sports team or NASCAR driver. In all of these instances, there is a sense that this "thing" has "something" and that I'll get it if I could just have that thing. I'll somehow be a Lexus kind of person or a Boston Red Sox kind of person. Percy's idea here is that I have a sense of my lacking something, something that this thing can fill. So I buy it.

But soon the magic wears off. The shoes, the gadget, the car, the "right" group of friends, the thing that I was so sure would really help me to "be somebody" (and for a brief time seemed to do just that), becomes humdrum. It becomes just another old pair of shoes, or car, or girlfriend. To Percy, it is as if I am a black hole, sucking the "it-ness" out of things. That Lexus was really something until I purchased it, and then it got sucked into the emptiness that is myself. Now it doesn't have any meaning, any transcendence, any "it" at all, just like me.

So I need to go get something new. Fashion, from clothes to cars to relationships, exists because of this idea.

---

1. Percy, *The Message in a Bottle*, 287.
2. Percy, *Lost in the Cosmos*, 181.

This is the "nought" that Percy is talking about. I am a zero, a nothingness that is always hungry and never filled. I am always somehow insubstantial and always looking to find substance. Percy makes his case with relentless thoroughness. Let's consider celebrity. We idolize rock stars, athletes, and movie stars. We copy their "look." They tell us in commercials that they drink this sports drink or that soda, so we do, too. Even though much of their public presentation is exactly that, a fabricated "presentation," we somehow feel like it is more "real" than we are.

Or consider achievement. We strive to "make something of ourselves," with the clear implication that right now there is no real self there. "If only I could make varsity . . ." "If I could get in that sorority . . ." "If I could land a job with that firm . . ." "If I could live in that city, marry that guy, have those friends . . ."

All of this is predicated upon the idea that being a self, something real and substantial, requires acquiring something that I don't now have. And yet that something proves maddeningly elusive. We think we've got it, and then it is gone. Earlier, I talked about the young woman I coached in track who won the long coveted state title, a goal she'd worked toward for years, and woke up the next morning to crushing depression. That kind of experience is what Percy is describing.

I'd like to suggest, as Percy himself hints, that while there is great cause for despair in such a situation, there is also hope. Coming to the end of the road, recognizing that it is a dead end and that one is lost, is the first step to getting going in the right direction. I think it is hopeful that the "nought" recognizes that it needs something beyond itself to be whole. The problem, really, is that the things that modern culture in the West teaches us to use to fill that emptiness only intensify the chasm in the long run. The hunger itself may actually prove to be a good thing. This is particularly true if it drives us to look in new places for that which can feed us.

I Was Afraid Because I Was Naked, So I Hid by Andrew Watson

PART THREE

Does God Leave Us There?

*C*HRISTIANS HAVE A TENDENCY *to leap from where we were last chapter,
looking at the reality of brokenness and sin in the world, all the way to
Jesus and the cross—almost as if two thousand years of the Old Testament
didn't happen or didn't matter. I'd like to sit in the Old Testament for a while,
for a couple reasons. For one thing, I believe God does not begin moving
to rescue and reconcile humanity when Jesus comes along. I believe that
process started almost as soon as sin enters our human experience in the
Garden. I'd like to tell part of that story. Another reason to spend some time
in the Old Testament is that this is where Jesus comes from; this is his history, his people, his story. So, while I propose to spend a bit of time telling
Old Testament stories, I believe I'm really telling Jesus stories. It's sort of
like someone coming up to me and saying, "Hey, tell me a little bit about
yourself, Steve. Who are you?" and I respond, "Well, to give you a picture of
who I am, I'll begin by telling you a story or two about my grandparents and
where they came from."*

*We too often look at Jesus as if he just plopped down from the sky and
landed in the manger in Bethlehem, with no history and no culture. He was
a Jew. That means something. He had an accent, particular ways of talking,
thinking, and living. He had a sense of humor and tastes in food that were
shaped by the family he grew up in and the town he was from. Yes, Jesus
is universally applicable, but before he's the Savior of the World, he was a
Jewish boy growing up in Nazareth. It might help us to understand him better if we knew some of the stories that shaped him and his people.*

Crying Out by Kelsey Vanden Hoek

Grace in the Midst of Barrenness

Muscle Memory and a Different Kind of Story

As we've discussed, once Adam and Eve fall in the garden, choosing self over openness to God, things go very badly very quickly. And they remain there. The story of the Bible, particularly the Old Testament, can read like one relentless cycle after another of people, individuals, and the nation of Israel, screwing things up. And not just in benign, "I made a bad choice" kinds of ways.

Why does God wait so long to take care of things? If God's endgame is for Jesus to come and save us, why doesn't it happen sooner? Why all the suffering in between?

Those are huge questions, and I don't want to suggest nor claim that I have a comprehensive answer for all of that. I do have an idea, however, that I think explains a good bit of what is going on in Israel's long, often painful relationship with God. In a nutshell, I believe God was shaping first Israel, and then all of humanity, into a kind of people that could comprehend who Jesus was and what he came to do. Another way of saying it would be that God was teaching us a language and a story that we would need for Jesus and his message (both in what he said and what he did) to make sense. Let me try to explain.

Earlier, I described the events of Adam and Eve in the Garden as taking instead of receiving with open hands, hiding in fear instead of relating openly, blaming instead of trusting and, finally, acting in violence toward one another instead of caring for one another. They were turning to God in fear and shame instead of facing God with open trust. That scene has been replayed until it has worn a grove into our ideas of what it means to be human, becoming *second nature*, literally. Our first response now to situations is to act like Adam and Eve. We seem to have no ability, the vast majority of the time, to even conceive of a way to live in which we don't strive to acquire, struggle with one another, and fight to protect what is ours.

Certainly this seems to be the case as we look at Israel's story in the Bible. As we shall see, in spite of the fact that they were born out of a helpless situation as slaves in Egypt and were rescued by God, Israel repeatedly acted as if their well-being was dependent upon their own militaristic efforts. In spite of the fact that God promised to care for them and guide them, they begged for a king, so they could be like all the other nations around them. The Old Testament is a collection of stories, really one story, of a people to whom God repeatedly says, "Open up your hands so I can give you gifts and blessings," who instead respond, "No, we've got to keep our fists clenched so we can take and hold on to what we need."

And, lest it seem like I'm being too hard on Israel, they really are just the Bible's example of how all of humanity functions, almost all the time. That is our story, too: Taking, wounding, hiding, and looking out for ourselves above all else. It is how we live and how we expect the world to work.

Jesus is God's answer to that story. The actions and teachings of Jesus show God to be a God who turns every facet of that story inside out. They show a definition of power that is demonstrated by service, self-sacrifice, and willingness to die for others. Everything about what Jesus says and does goes against everything that our world values and has valued for as long as anyone can possibly remember.

Given that, how are we to receive this Jesus? How can his message, in word and action, be even remotely intelligible to us? We run the danger of being so drenched in the story of the fall that we can't see the possibility of the world being anything but what we've come to know.

Have you ever seen the classic Christmas movie, *It's a Wonderful Life?* In it Jimmy Stewart's character, who has been a consistent force for good in his community his entire life, is convinced his life is ruined and wants to commit suicide. Before he can, an angel gives him a glimpse of what his town would be like if he had never been born. For several scenes, Stewart watches aghast as people he has grown up with, people who are good and kind friends and neighbors, live out an entirely different reality. In this world without Stewart, the town is dark and depressed, and its people are fearful, cynical, and angry. Stewart tries to talk to them and tell them of the town he knows and how they fit in it, but everyone he meets responds with confusion, disbelief, or anger. They have no frame of reference at all for the alternate world Stewart is describing.

Without the long history of God's interactions with humanity, first with one individual and his family and later with the nation of Israel, we would be in the same predicament as the townspeople in *It's a Wonderful*

Life. Jesus would come to us, and we would have no possible way to understand.

God spent all those years continuing to interact with stubborn and rarely faithful Israel. In the midst of Israel's (and our) story of taking, hiding, and violence, God is weaving a different story. To Abraham, essentially saying, "You will not be able to maintain this covenant. I will do it for you." To the Israelites enslaved in Egypt, "I have heard your cry and have come to rescue you." Again to Israel communicating in action the message, "These sacrifices are a gift to you. To heal you." Over and over as Israel goes to war, victory is *never* a matter of winning by superior might. Whenever Israel has success, it is because they are woefully outnumbered, and God miraculously delivers them. Again and again, children are born in the biblical story to women who are too old (Abraham's wife, Sarah), are unable to conceive (Elizabeth), or are virgins (Jesus' mother, Mary).

Whether it is physical barrenness in the case of the repeated miraculous pregnancies or the metaphoric barrenness of God rescuing people who have no hope on their own, God provides grace and mercy. One of my favorite professors in seminary, Ray Anderson, described it this way: God is teaching Israel a counter-story. Instead of a story of "might makes right" and "if you want it, you better grab it for yourself," God is teaching a story in which God says, "In your barrenness, I will provide My grace." Anderson said, "God's grace presupposes (or assumes) human barrenness." Let me put it this way: God, in effect, says to us, "How can I give you my grace, my mercy and provision, when your fists are clinched to take and to hurt? Open your hands and let me fill them."

In sports or music, people talk about muscle memory. Muscle memory is the idea that no matter how gifted Tiger Woods or Lebron James may be, without hour after hour of repeating practice golf swings or twenty-foot jump shots, they would not be the athletes they are. The thousands upon thousands of practice swings and shots groove into their muscles and minds what it takes to be able to perform without thinking. So, when the moment of truth comes, on the eighteenth fairway of the Masters or the seventh game of a championship series, they don't have to think, "How do I do this?" It just comes.

Likewise with musicians, an elite level violinist or pianist is born with phenomenal skill, but he or she also spend hours upon hours practicing. And not just practicing the most difficult pieces of music, but hours practicing the basics, the rudimentary scales and drills that form the building blocks of being a world-class musician. They are developing muscle memory, so that when they sit on stage in Carnegie Hall, they don't have to think about every little note. They just play.

I don't think even the most optimistic among us would dispute that our "muscle memory" has plenty of the fall woven into who we are. We don't have to think about how to take from one another. We don't have to think about how to respond in anger or to turn from God. It comes without effort. Some would argue that we are so damaged that we can't even recognize goodness and grace when it arrives in front of us. We are so tainted that we lack the ability to see Jesus or comprehend his utterly transforming message and deeds.

We need new muscle memories. We need a new story. That's why God takes so long. Through all of these centuries and in the midst of all the sin and violence, God is telling a different story, giving us a different experience. God is slowly and patiently teaching Israel (and hopefully us) how to recognize grace when they see it. Even when their fists are clinched for years upon years, they are reminded, "Open them up. I promise you you'll be glad you did. This is what you need." The hope being that—when grace truly appears, not just in acts of mercy but in a person, Jesus—they, and we, might recognize him and know how to respond.

A Strange Scene That Is the Key to the Whole Story

EVERY GOOD STORY HAS plot twists, moments where the story takes a new and unexpected turn. Perhaps a new character is introduced or a new circumstance changes everything. God's story of interacting with humanity, the Bible, is no different. Reading the Bible a few thousand years after much of it was written makes all of it a bit foreign or strange to us. In some ways, we have to piece together or guess at an earlier culture every time we read the Bible. The early stories of scripture, in particular, seem shrouded in mystery. Some scholars, in fact, talk about the first large chunk of Genesis being humanity's *prehistory*. That is not to say that these events in the Bible are pre-true or just legends. It is more to say that they are from a period when cultures were not yet recording their stories as histories. The few other stories that exist from other cultures or religions that date back to this time are more mythological than historical.

Some of the early stories of the Bible read this way, as well. Again, that's not to say they are not historically true, but they read like myths—talking serpents, people living for hundreds of years, a great flood destroying all of the earth except for a select few.

And then there is this story.

Through the first eleven chapters of Genesis, God interacts with humanity, but only sporadically. After the Fall (Adam and Eve taking the fruit forbidden them, they become aware of themselves and their nakedness, their hiding from God), God no longer relates to specific people on an ongoing basis. He appears from time to time, but nothing like a relationship is going on for chapter after chapter and, very likely, century after century.

And then, in chapter twelve, God comes to one man, Abram (whose name will soon be changed to the name many are more likely to know, Abraham) and gives him instructions to pick up from where he's living with his clan and go to a new place that will be given especially to him. Additionally, God will make him a great nation (he'll have a large and powerful family). God will especially bless Abraham and his descendents, and they will, in turn, be a blessing to the whole world. He promises to bless them and protect them. Abraham is already very old, as is his wife, and they have no children, but God promises to give them a son.

A few things are important to note before going any further. First, Abram/Abraham has not asked for this blessing. There is no hint in the story that he even had any sense of God. God just chooses him. God initiates the contact. Second, aside from asking Abraham to leave the land of his ancestors and go where God will take him, God asks nothing of Abraham, but God promises to *do* quite a bit on Abraham's behalf. God is initiating and God is blessing. Finally, this choosing one person and promising to uniquely bless him might seem pretty capricious on God's part. What about everyone else? Does God love only a few? This has been a troubling question for people ever since. In the Old Testament, does God love only the nation of Israel (Abraham's descendents)? In the New Testament and beyond, does God love only Christians? We ask this because we have failed to pay attention to the entire blessing given to Abraham.

"I will bless you ... and *all peoples on earth will be blessed through you.*"[1]

Throughout their history, Israel tended to forget the second half of the promise. They were clear on the point that they were God's Chosen People, but not so keen on recognizing that the point of their being chosen was to be God's conduit (others blessed *through* them) through which all of humanity would be blessed. They're not alone, however. In many ways, Christianity has done the same thing. Many Christians seem to believe that God loves Christians uniquely, not like Abraham, as God's unique instrument of blessing to the world (which Christians are meant to be), but as God's *only* beloved ones.

Back to the story. Abraham and Sarah are *really old.* Abraham is one hundred years old and Sarah is ninety. Their years of potentially having children are long past. They are very aware of this. They come up with plans for how *they* can help God's promise come true. They suggest to God that the blessing could come through Abraham's nephew. Then Abraham sleeps with one of his slaves and impregnates her (at one hundred, a semi-miraculous event in itself) and suggests that the boy, Ishmael, be the answer to the promise. God says, "No." Abraham's effort cannot bring the blessing. Only God's gift can bring it. This reality will repeat itself over and over throughout the Bible and is one of *the* central realities of God's

---

1. Genesis 12:2–3.

story. Humanity cannot help itself, and God acts on its behalf as sheer gift. The baby, Isaac, eventually comes, and his life is God's gift to Abraham and Sarah.

Before Isaac is born, God intensifies the relationship with Abraham. In Genesis 15, an event takes place that truly is strange and mysterious and yet is of colossal importance. God again comes to Abraham and repeats the promise that Abraham and Sarah will have a son. In fact, God instructs Abraham to look to the heavens, for his offspring will be more numerous than the stars; he will live in a blessed and prosperous land. Abraham asks how he can be sure that this is really going to happen. This is where things get weird.

God instructs Abraham to kill a cow, a goat, a ram, a dove, and a pigeon and cut their bodies in two. He is next to lay their carcasses on the ground with a gap between them. Abraham does all of this and then proceeds to fall into a sleep/stupor. In this state, he witnesses a smoking firepot and a blazing torch appearing before him and then pass between the split carcasses. He also hears God's voice, repeating the promised blessing.

Reading this story thousands of years after it happens, it is natural to be confused and perhaps a little repulsed. This is a gruesome, bizarre event. A bit of historical context takes away much of the strangeness. In ancient civilizations, suzerain/vassal covenants were a common occurrence. A suzerain would be the dominant king or tribal lord, and a vassal would be the weaker king or lord. The suzerain would set the terms of the covenant, or deeply binding contract. He (suzerains invariably were men) would dictate what blessings he was willing to give to the weaker vassal, and he would list what was expected in return. Typically, as is true in most human power relationships, the powerful party gave much less than he demanded in return. The vassal was not there to negotiate. He was there to accept whatever the suzerain was willing to give and agree to whatever demands were made.

Finally, after the stating of conditions, the vassal, the weaker party, *would be made to walk between the slaughtered animals.* This action was highly symbolic. In passing between the animals, the vassal was, in effect, saying, "Let it be done to me as it has been done to these animals if I fail to keep the covenant." The stronger party set the rules. He determined what he was willing to give, what he demanded in return, and what the punishment would be if the weaker party failed.

That is what is happening here in Genesis 15, with one huge and striking exception. Abraham is clearly the weaker party. It is he that should pass between the animals. But he doesn't. He watches the pot and torch pass between them. What is happening here? The pot and torch represent God. God is taking on the burden of maintaining the covenant. Rather than requiring Abraham to state by his actions, "Let it be to me as it is to these animals if the covenant is broken," God is bearing that responsibility.

This is the key to everything that follows in the Bible and in our experience with God. God has promised a blessing to Abraham: A miraculous gift that will come to a couple who can do nothing for themselves but must depend only upon God's gift of life. This blessing is for Abraham, but not for him alone. God's gift of grace comes to him so that it will then pass on to all of humanity. Finally, as God forms a new relationship with Abraham, as representative of all of humanity, God takes on the burden of responsibility if the covenant is broken.

God knows what is coming. Abraham will not keep the covenant. Israel, his descendants, will not. We will not. And God will truly keep the promise: "Let it be to me as it is to these animals if the covenant is broken." On the cross, God keeps the promise made centuries upon centuries before. God bears the responsibility that rightfully should have been Abraham's, Israel's, and ours.

A God Who Hears and Acts

EVERY NATION HAS A founding story. It is grounded in truth but also shrouded in myth and legend. It is a story of heroes and heroines in which they fight against all odds to overcome evil and establish a home, a place of freedom and goodness. Look at the story here in the United States. Faced with unbearable oppression by the evil British Empire (they were taxing us more than we wanted, after all!), a small band of ragtag colonialists, led by the heroic George Washington, fought against overwhelming odds and won our freedom. From those brave deeds came the greatest nation the world has ever known. The beacon of freedom and democracy, goodness and justice, a City on the Hill!

Now, I left out the parts about our really being pretty lucky in that war and how, if the French and Prussians hadn't come to our aid, we likely never would have had a chance and how, at least to some degree, England just grew tired of fighting an unpopular war and pulled out as much as we conquered them or that as we won "our" freedom we also took the freedom of the peoples who were already living here on the continent and those we brought from Africa to help build our prosperity. But isn't the way I told it pretty much the way we, and really every country, tells its story? Don't worry about the parts that aren't brave and noble and heroic. Highlight the parts that are.

I don't mean to turn this into a discourse on U.S. history. My reason for telling this story is to point out that Israel, the nation from which Jesus comes, has a *very* different kind of story. The contrast between their story and the ones that pretty much everyone else tells is fascinating and telling about what kind of people they are and what kind of God they are dealing with. We spent a bit of time earlier looking at this story, God's deliverance of the Israelites from slavery in Egypt, but I'd like to return to it again.

To review what we discussed earlier, a few generations after Abraham and God's remarkable covenant with him, Abraham's clan, now grown quite large, ends up living in Egypt. They live there for four hundred years. During that time, they become a vast people, so much so that the Egyptians, who four hundred years earlier had welcomed them as guests, now resent them and fear their ever-growing numbers. So they enslave them, brutally. The opening pages of Exodus tell of the oppressive labor conditions Pharaoh forces upon the Israelites. It talks of a "bitter life" for the Israelites as they are treated "harshly" and "ruthlessly." The Israelites groan in their suffering.

And God hears them.

In Exodus 3, God says to Moses, a Jew raised in Pharaoh's household and now on the run from Pharaoh, "I [God speaking to Moses] have seen the misery of my people who are in Egypt; I have heard them crying out on account of their slave drivers, and I am concerned about their sufferings. So I have come down to rescue them . . ."[1] I would like to highlight a few phrases from that statement.

> I have indeed *seen the misery of my people . . .*
> I have *heard them crying out . . .*
> I am *concerned . . .*
> I have *come down to rescue them . . .*

In the worlds of ancient religions, gods were distant and mysterious, even frightening, figures. One never knew what the gods wanted, how to please them, or how to get them to intervene on one's behalf. The gods did as they pleased, perhaps intervening on their people's behalf, but just as likely not. In a word, the gods were capricious.

And here is Israel's God. He hears them, is concerned for them, and most important, *comes down to rescue them.* What follows is the story of plagues, angels of death, the parting of the Red Sea, and miraculous deliverance. Older generations knew the story from the Charlton Heston film *The Ten Commandments,* while my children know the Disney film, *Moses, Prince of Egypt.* What we have in both, though, is Israel's founding story. Theirs is not a tale of their own bravery and resourcefulness. Theirs is not a tale of fighting gallantly against overwhelming odds.

Let me summarize the Israelites' founding story. Theirs is a story of being hopelessly bound in slavery. Theirs is a story of having no ability to rescue themselves. Theirs is a story of a God who sees them, hears them crying out, and *comes to rescue* them. That is a *very* different kind of founding story. It is not a pull-yourself-up-by-your-bootstraps kind of story that we in America like so much. It is a we-were-helpless-and-a-helper-came-to-rescue-us story.

---

1. Exodus 3:7–8.

To this day, observant Jews, thousands of years after the events of the Exodus, celebrate this story every Passover. They celebrate a meal together. This is their Fourth of July. Before the meal, the youngest male at the table asks the oldest male, "Why is this night different from every other?" and the oldest male tells, again, the story that all of them know, the story that shapes who they are. We are a helpless people, but we have a God who hears and who acts to rescue.

What if we saw their story as also ours?

Tabernacle

IT CAN BE TEMPTING to think that God becoming flesh in Jesus is a new idea for God that just crops up in the New Testament. We may think that, somehow, God had previously left us on our own but now decides to get involved. While there are unique things about how God gets involved in the coming of Jesus to be with us, it would be a mistake to see this as something new in the mind of God. God has *always* been a God who, when faced with the suffering of humanity, enters in and dwells with. This is God's nature. It is not a whim or an accident (something God didn't need to do but just chooses to do) that God enters into human suffering. To do so is who God is.

As we just noted, God had come and acted in a tangible way to rescue Israel from slavery in Egypt. What happens next makes the point of God's entering-in-and-dwelling-with nature. After leaving Egypt, God takes the Israelites to nearby Mount Sinai where he gives Moses the Law (the Ten Commandments are part of this, but just a part; the Law received here is a vast set of instructions on how to live as God's people). At the end of this extensive list of ordinances and instructions, God tells them to build a vast tent. In fact, God goes into page after page of details about what this tent should look like. As a kid growing up in church, I thought this part of the Bible was unbearably boring. I know better now.

Here is what is going on.

God knows something that Moses and the people do not know. They believe they are just a few short weeks from entering the Promised Land, a land that God has said would be their home and a place of peace and blessing. What they don't know is that when they arrive there, they will chicken out. There will be people in the land, and the Israelites will be afraid of them and will ask God to let them go back to Egypt. As a result of this and numerous other acts of faithless disobedience, they will spend the next forty years wandering in a desert that they should have been able to cross in less than a month. Other than two of them, the only two who believed God would give them the Promised Land, all of them will die in the wilderness.

This is grim stuff! The Israelites have hopped from the frying pan into the fire, as it were. Sure, God rescued them from slavery, but this almost seems worse. And in real ways, it is. It is a disaster. This is why the big tent is so important.

The big tent is the Tabernacle. When it is complete, God says that he intends to dwell there as the people wander in the wilderness. "I will dwell among the Israelites and be their God. They will know that I am the Lord their God, who brought them out of Egypt so that I might dwell among them."[1]

Does the sin of Israel have consequences? Yes, forty years of suffering and death in the wilderness. And where is God as they suffer? "Build me a tent. As you head off into the wilderness, to suffer and to die, I am coming with you." This is their God, a God who is with them.

When Jesus comes, Matthew says that he shall be called *Emmanuel*, meaning "God with us." Is this a new idea? The Jews of Jesus' time would not think so. This is the God they have always known.

Theologians call this event, this God-coming-in-Jesus, the Incarnation. What does that mean?

Have you ever eaten chili con carne? If so, you are familiar with the idea of the Incarnation. Chili con carne is "chili with meat." The Incarnation is "God with meat." The Incarnation is God with flesh. It is God entering in. In the wilderness, God dwelt in a tent. In the New Testament, this "being with you" nature of God takes on the shape of a person. In both cases, this is not a strategy God employs; it is an expression of God's nature. God is a God who enters in, walks with us in our lives and in our suffering.

One of the great questions of humanity is "Where is God in our suffering?" As millions of Jews were sent to the ovens of the Holocaust, or as a young child is abused and murdered, or as a beloved mother dies of breast cancer, where is God? This question is not asked abstractly. It is often accompanied by intense anguish and pain. The question of God's place in human suffering is complex and in some ways larger than the scope of this little book. *But*, I feel confident in saying that, while I don't know all of *what* God is doing when we suffer, I think I know *where* God is during those times. God is present with us.

---

1. Exodus 29:45–46.

God Present at the Concord, Massachusetts, Hospital

MY MOST VIVID EXPERIENCE of this happened in the winter of 1992. I had taken a few Young Life guys skiing on President's Day, which was a day off from school. Al, an avid skier, had sat out almost the whole afternoon, and everyone in the car was teasing him about it on the drive home from Vermont. He said he just wasn't feeling very good. Within two days, Al was in the hospital with pneumonia. He was supposed to be there just a few days. I stopped by the hospital on Thursday thinking, "If I don't get there today, he'll check out and I'll be able to see him at his home." When I arrived, Al wasn't in his room. I thought he'd checked out but I was quickly told he'd been moved to Intensive Care. A few hours earlier, Al had gone into a rare condition called Adult Respiratory Distress Syndrome (ARDS). ARDS is sort of a heart attack for the lungs. They had just shut down. Al was now in a coma, kept alive by a ventilator.

Al's family allowed me to come back into the unit (only family and very few others were there), and that began the longest, most intense week of my life. For the next week, I spent about fourteen to sixteen hours a day at that hospital. Al had many friends, and very quickly they too began arriving in droves. Most weren't allowed past the hospital lobby, but they came anyway. Dozens at a time would sit and whisper together and pray for Al.

Al's parents and older sister almost never left the unit. They slept there, ate there. Strangely, I stumbled into the role of being one of the couple of people who communicated Al's condition and the family's feelings to the high school students in the hospital lobby and at the school he attended. Al's condition was largely signified by a monitor that sat to the right of his head. It had a number that registered the amount of oxygen in Al's bloodstream. A number in the eighties is healthy; brain damage occurs when the number stays for very long in the fifties. Al started the week just below seventy, and as the week went on that number drifted up and down but mostly down, eventually settling around fifty. As the week progressed, I would call the school every few hours with an update on the current number, and it would be posted on the window of the main office. A lot of people were very concerned about Al.

The emotions of that week were remarkably intense. One of the ones I still recall most palpably was walking down the long corridor from Al's room to the lobby several times a day wondering what in the world to tell the assembled kids there. I wanted to be upbeat. I wanted to give them a sense that God heard their prayers and that miracles can and do happen. I also wanted to be honest with them that the numbers were slowly dipping lower and lower. I did not want to hide from them that things did not look hopeful. I had no idea what to say. I just prayed and prayed. I prayed for a miracle or some sort of insight as to what to say in the absence of one.

For most of the week, I heard nothing. On Thursday night, I was again walking down that corridor. Again begging God to do something decisive, to provide a miracle. I wanted God to provide a voice. I wanted God to somehow make this horrific scene go away. And God answered, but in none of those ways.

In a way I have struggled for years to find words for, I sensed God's answer. It was just, "I am here." Not, "I am here, and here's what I'm going to do," or "I am here, and here is how this will all play out." Just, "I am here. I am present." It was at once one of the most terrifying sensations I have ever had and the most comforting. I still didn't know if Al would live or die or what in the world I'd say in ninety seconds when I turned the corner into the lobby, but I knew to the depth of my being that God was present with Al, with his parents, with all the kids in the lobby, and with me.

Al died the next night, while being transported from the Boston suburban hospital where he'd been to one of the world's leading hospitals downtown. His funeral was attended by hundreds on a brutally cold Massachusetts winter morning and was one of the most powerful experiences I have ever had. For the next year, a good-sized group of Al's friends and a couple of Young Life leaders had spaghetti dinner every Wednesday night with Al's parents, Maureen and big Al, because spaghetti night had been Al's favorite night of the week.

Where was God as the Israelites suffered in the wilderness? Where was God as the Jews faced the Holocaust? He was in the heat and sand with them. He was in the gas chambers of Auschwitz.

Al's Story, Part Two

A VERY STRANGE AND beautiful thing happened in the aftermath of Al's death. Al's family was Christian—Protestant Congregationalists. A woman who taught elementary school with Al's mom was Catholic. There was a Benedictine Monastery on the edge of Harvard, Massachusetts, the town next to Al's. This woman called the monks there and asked them to pray for Al when he went into a coma. They did. And they did much more.

These monks had no connection to Al's family. They were Catholic and Al's family was not. They were monks that rarely left the monastery and had very limited interactions with anyone in the community. Still, a handful of them came to the hospital, met Al's family, and prayed for Al there. They also noticed all of the kids in the lobby.

The day after Al died, the head Abbot at the monastery called Al's parents and invited all of the Young Life kids, and anyone else who would want to come, to join them for Evening Prayers (Vespers) and dinner that Sunday. A few dozen teenagers, none of whom had ever set foot on the grounds of this monastery and many of whom had never set foot in a church, spent that Sunday evening being fed by, sung to, prayed for, and embraced by a group of middle-aged and elderly men in black robes. Many of those young people, months and years later, described that evening as the most healing thing that happened in the aftermath of Al's death.

What Do You See?

GOD IS NOWHERE

A Couple of Interesting Hebrew Words

tsedeqah: righteousness
>> What we typically think of when we think of righteousness:
>>> upright living, pure behavior.
>>> For example: not drinking or smoking, abstaining from
>>> pre- or extra-marital sex, or reading the Bible every day.
>> What the word means:
>>> being in right relationship.
>>> Behaviors like the ones listed above may be signs of
>>> righteousness, but
>>> righteousness, *tsedeqah,* is a relational term.

shalom: peace
>> What we think of tends to be merely, peace:
>>> the absence of violence.
>> What the word more fully means:
>>> wholeness, things as they should be. It's an all-
>>> encompassing idea.
>>> The absence of violence is part of it, but the word means
>>> so much more.
>>> Jesus, Prince of Peace, is really, Jesus, Prince of Shalom
>>> (Prince of wholeness, Prince of things as they should
>>> be).

We are people lacking in both *tsedeqah* and *shalom.* We stand before God as unrighteous, and we think of this as standing before a judge, having violated the rules. What we mostly have done is violated "right *relationship.*" We are people of "things that should not be."

We need a way back into the reality of these words, *tsedeqah* and *shalom.* This is the story God is telling.

Our Story and God's Counter-Story

Judges and Ruth

Aㅤ FTER FORTY YEARS OF Israel's wandering and suffering in the wilderness and many more years taking and settling into the land, Judges tells us the story of how Israel lives in "the Promised Land." Before the book begins, the people of Israel have renewed their covenantal vows with God. Their leader, Joshua, before his death reminds them of how God had delivered them from slavery in Egypt and cared for them over the years. He reminds them of the Law that gives form and shape to their relationship with God. He asks them if they will follow God after he dies or not. To a person, they vow to walk in relationship and obedience with God.

In that context, the book of Judges is shocking. While there are isolated moments of faithfulness, harmony, and peace, most of the time there is violence, idolatry, and wickedness. The *judges*, from whom the book derives its name, are men and women whom God "raises up" to rescue the people when their situations become most dire, but even many of them are far from shining moral examples.

The most famous, Samson, is a case in point. While he possesses great strength and God uses him to deliver the people of Israel from their enemy, the Philistines, Samson seems to have no impulse control whatsoever. He chases after women. He thinks nothing about killing dozens just to avenge slights and personal offenses. He is violent and arrogant. He squanders God's gift of strength to him and, though still fulfilling God's purpose in "raising him up," destroys himself in the process.

Another figure, a Levite and a priest, is at the center of a horrific tale of gang rape, murder, mutilation, and revenge on a scale that leaves tens of thousands dead. He responds callously to the rape and murder of his concubine (a sort of common-law wife in the ancient world—part wife, part servant). Instead of showing compassion to her, he cuts her body into twelve pieces and uses each to call the tribes of Israel to arms against their own kinsman, the Benjamites, some who had raped and killed her. The resulting bloodshed leaves over twenty thousand Benjamites dead and only a few hundred alive.

These men, and stories like these, are the norm for the Israelites in the book of Judges. If there was any need to demonstrate the ruinous effects of the fall in Genesis 3, the book of Judges paints, by and large, a nightmarish picture. A recurring phrase in the book is, "There was no king in the land and everyone did what was right in their own eyes." This is both a statement about what would come later, that God would allow them to have a king, but also a statement about Israel and God. The idea had been that Israel would not need a king because they had God. God would lead them, care for them, and provide for them if they would only look to God and follow. But, just as we saw with Adam and Eve and continuing until today, each one "does what was right in their own eyes." The result is just as horrific, only now played out on a national, instead of individual, scale.

This is humanity's story. This is our muscle memory, the tune we know so well, playing itself out in grisly detail. And in the middle of this, God's counter-story, God's counter-melody, pulses on.

The first words in the book of Ruth are, "In the days of the Judges . . ." And thus starts a very different story.

Ruth is a gentile, the daughter-in-law of a Jewish widow, Naomi. In the first pages of the story, Ruth's husband, Naomi's son, dies. Now they are both widows. Naomi has lost both her son and her husband. This would be a tragic turn of events in any age and culture, but at this time, it is a disaster. In the ancient world, women were completely dependent upon men for financial security. Only men could own property. A woman could be secure if she were the daughter of a living father, the wife of a husband, or a mother of a son. Naomi is now none of these. She is facing utter ruin.

She urges Ruth to leave her, to leave their Jewish home and go back to her gentile home. Ruth is young, and as we will see, very likely attractive. She can find a new husband. She, at least, has some hope.

Except that she refuses to leave. "Where you go, I will go. Your people will be my people and your God will be my God,"[1] is Ruth's response to Naomi. Essentially, it means "I will not abandon you to starve alone. I will starve with you." Already, this doesn't sound like the rest of the stories we see in Judges.

---

1. Ruth 1:16.

As they begin to make their way in the world, Naomi remembers a distant relative, Boaz, who is a wealthy landowner. She sends Ruth out to his fields. The Law God had given Israel had multiple provisions for caring for the poor. One related to harvesting the fields. As harvesting was done by hand, it was only natural that, as harvesters walked along, a fair bit of grain would fall to the ground. Rather than returning to scoop it up, the Israelites were to leave the scraps where they fell so that the poor could come behind and gather what they could. A second note in God's counter-melody sounds as Ruth gathers food according to Jewish Law to help Naomi and herself survive.

Boaz, perhaps just because of goodness of heart and perhaps because of Ruth's attractiveness, takes notice. He instructs his workers not only to let Ruth gather, but also to actually drop extra so that she will have more to collect. While not yet publicly acting on their behalf, Boaz is choosing to work for the good of Naomi and Ruth.

At last, Naomi decides it is time to reveal to Ruth and Boaz that they are related. In a scene that is confusing to us in our culture, Ruth puts herself at Boaz' feet as he sleeps, covering his feet and appealing to his mercy and protection (like I said, it's an odd scene, for which we don't have an easy comparison). When he awakes, he promises to care for Ruth and Naomi in a permanent way. This will mean either getting Naomi's closest male relative to buy the land Naomi's husband had owned and marry Ruth or to do so himself if this relative is not willing. When the other relative declines, Boaz buys the land and marries Ruth.

He is what the Bible calls their *kinsman redeemer*. Again, this is an idea from the Law given to Israel to care for widows in need. Given the precarious status of unmarried women, it was the expectation that the nearest male relative would *redeem* the woman by either marrying her, buying her dead husband's property, or taking her into his home.

Here is a relative who has come to the aid and rescue of one who could not rescue herself. Here is God's counter-story, working its way through the violent, anti-God story going on around Ruth and Boaz.

A relative, acting in mercy and care to rescue the helpless: Work this story into your muscle memory, Israel. It's going to come back around again, only on a much grander scale.

Jonah: Not the Story You Think You Know

O NE OF THE BEST-KNOWN and least understood stories in scripture is the story of Jonah. I teach a freshmen Bible Survey class every year at George Fox University, and one of my favorite things to do is introduce the discussion of Jonah by asking the class, "What's the point of this story? Who is this story about? What's the climax of the story?" Invariably, most of the class answers, "Well, clearly the story is about Jonah and how he learned to be obedient. The key moment is when Jonah is vomited up by the fish and then obeys God's instructions." The trap has been sprung! I'll smile mischievously and say, "Well, maybe you're right. Let's take a look at it."

Jonah may well be the most ironic, satirical book of the Bible. It is loaded with surprises. Virtually none of the characters in the story do what they are supposed to do. Let me summarize the plot. Nineveh, the Assyrian capital, is exceedingly wicked, and God calls upon Jonah to go and prophesy to it that God's wrath is about to fall upon the city. Jonah has no interest in prophesying to them, whether from fear or hatred of the nation that will soon destroy Israel, so he runs away, getting on a ship going the opposite direction. God sends a huge storm to slow him down. The pagan sailors in the ship recognize that God or the gods are angry and ask Jonah what he thinks. Jonah knows his disobedience is the cause of the storm and encourages the sailors to save themselves by chucking him overboard. The pagan sailors will have none of that and desperately try to row the ship back to shore, but are unable and finally consent to chucking Jonah, whereupon the storm ceases. The sailors worship God, and Jonah sinks toward his death. God sends a huge fish (the whale in most of our imaginations) to save Jonah by swallowing him.

Inside the fish, Jonah, strangely enough, worships God. The fish spits Jonah out, and he finally sets off to Nineveh to do what God has asked of him. Nineveh is a huge city, requiring three days to walk from one end to the other. Jonah walks into it for one day and makes a one-sentence pronouncement, "Thirty days and Nineveh will be no more." Job completed, he exits the city and takes a seat on a nearby hill to watch God's destruction rain down on Israel's enemy.

Stunningly, all of Nineveh repents. They mourn over their sin. They fast. From king to commoner, the whole city responds to Jonah's message. And God responds to them. He forgives them. He has mercy upon them and calls off their destruction.

Jonah is incensed! Jonah explains that the reason he tried to run away was that, "I knew that you were a gracious and compassionate God, slow to anger and abounding in love. Take my life!"

God doesn't take his life but sends a plant to grow up overnight and give Jonah shade as he sits in the desert sun. Jonah loves the shade and, therefore, loves the plant. The next day, however, a bug eats the root of the plant, and it withers in the sun. Jonah mourns the death of his beloved plant that had given him a day's worth of shade. He again calls upon God to kill him.

The story ends with God's response: "You have been concerned about this gourd, though you did not tend it or make it grow . . . Should I not have concern for the great city of Nineveh in which there are more than a hundred and twenty thousand people who cannot tell their right hand from their left—and also many animals?"

Now, as a class, we begin to discuss the story. There are a lot of pagans, or Gentiles, in this story. How do they act? What do they do? Well, they all, from the sailors to the people of Nineveh, seem receptive to God and either repent or worship God.

How does the one Jew, the representative of God's chosen people, respond? He first disobeys, then grudgingly obeys, and then is furious at God's mercy.

How does God act? He gives mercy. God gives mercy to the sailors, to Jonah, to the people of Nineveh. Is Jonah the hero of the story? If so, it is only as some sort of antihero in contrast to God. Jonah literally says, "I would rather die, God, than live in a world where you have mercy on my enemies!"

Who is the hero of the story? God. What is the climax of the story? The climax is God's question at the end: "You are sad about the death of the plant, and yet you think it's wrong that I be moved with compassion toward this entire city?"

What a wild story! It has Gentiles following God. It's got a Jewish prophet disobedient and with a hardened heart. It includes a fish that swallows Jonah, not as a punishment, but as an act of mercy on God's part. And, most important, it showcases a God who has mercy from first to last. Jonah is the only book in the Bible that ends with a question, and what a question it is. It contrasts our mercy with God's. If any of us knew the brutality of Assyria as Jonah did, we'd understand why he was upset that Nineveh had been spared. He's not so much an evil person as he is a person just like all of us. That's the core of God's closing question to him. "Don't you see that I am not like you? Don't you see how much more vast is my mercy and love than yours?"

On Judgment, Wrath, and God

WE'VE TALKED A GOOD bit in the last few chapters about sin and brokenness. What does God have to say about that? Isn't a lot of the Bible filled with God's wrath toward people like us? Isn't God often talked about in the Bible as being angry and judging?

Here's an example from Paul's letter to the church in Rome: "But because of your stubbornness and unrepentant heart, you are storing up wrath against yourself for the day of God's wrath, when his righteous judgment will be revealed . . ."[1] Storing up wrath, day of God's wrath, righteous judgment. Does this sound like the infinitely compassionate God I described in the first section? It certainly does not on the surface. To help make sense of this, I'd like to draw two contrasting views of justice: judgment and wrath.

For years, I had quite a lead foot when driving. My wife and I lived in the Midwest. I did a lot of driving on long, straight highways, and I was often in a hurry. One time in particular, I was in a meeting in Chicago that lasted deep into the afternoon, and I had scheduled another meeting in the evening back in Iowa City, a three-and-a-half-hour drive away. I had rented a car to drive to the Chicago meeting and, as I often did, had stayed too long in Chicago, talking to friends. I left three hours before the meeting in Iowa City was supposed to start.

I had to make up some time, and I was doing just that. I was without a doubt driving quite a bit over the speed limit. In fact, every time I checked, I was hovering around 80 miles per hour. About two hours into the drive, just before crossing the Mississippi River into Iowa, I looked in my rearview mirror and saw the dreaded flashing lights of an Illinois State Trooper. As they usually do, the officer asked me if I knew how fast I'd been driving. I knew I'd been driving a little over 80, and I didn't think I'd gone faster than that. I decided I was going to own up to my guilt and say, "Yes sir, I was driving right at or just over 80."

He was not impressed with my honesty. He said, "Some of the time. I clocked you 10 miles back driving 102 miles per hour. I am writing you

---

1. Romans 2:5.

81

a ticket for driving 102. You have a court date for next month where you will either pay a four hundred dollar fine or have your license revoked."

What?! I'd never driven that fast in my life and did not think I had this time. Trying my best to be as respectful as possible, I said, "Sir, are you sure there's not some mistake? I am in a rental car, and perhaps the speedometer is not accurate. While I knew I was speeding, I've been watching the speedometer, and I never saw it over 80."

His reply. "I am writing you a ticket for driving 102 miles per hour. You have a court date for next month where you will either pay a four hundred dollar fine or have your license revoked."

A month later, I was sitting in the Dixon, Illinois, courthouse waiting for my case to come up. With me that morning were men on trial for domestic battery, possession of marijuana, and a fight in a bar, and me, the prodigal speeder. When my turn came, I approached the bench, and when asked by the judge to speak, told my story of being late for a meeting (which I casually mentioned was a Christian youth ministry meeting where I would be bringing the message of Jesus to needy young people, hoping for a little sympathy there), how I'd been in a rental car that clearly had a faulty speedometer, and how I was sure I hadn't been driving over 80 or so (which I knew was way too fast and which I promised never to do again).

The judge said, "Mr. Sherwood, I think it's super that you work to help young people, but the officer gave you a ticket for driving more than one hundred miles per hour, and you need to pay the clerk four hundred dollars today before leaving or your license will be revoked. Driving at that speed is dangerous to yourself and others and is a menace to public safety."

This was blind justice. The judge was doing his job. He was not supposed to decide if I seemed trustworthy or sympathetic. There is a legal code, and he was commissioned to make sure it was followed and, when not followed, to mete out the appropriate punishment. He scolded me, not because he knew or cared anything about me, but because he cared about the code of justice and I had violated it. In a very real sense, he was blind to me as a person. He saw only the Law and my breaking of it. It's no accident that the symbol of justice is a blindfolded woman holding a scale. This kind of justice and the wrath and judgment that comes with it are not supposed to be personal in any way. Justice is not supposed to see the person at all. It just sees the rules and whether or not they are kept.

When most of us read verses in the Bible about God's wrath toward injustice or our misdeeds, this is what we picture. We picture God impassively comparing our lives unfavorably to a cosmic code of law and, because we are found lacking in that comparison, reacting in judgment. But this isn't the only possibility.

My two daughters have a few similarly aged girlfriends who live in our neighborhood, and they often play together in our backyard. I'll often overhear them. Being kids, and being human, there are often problems. One or another of them will not share well, will take too many turns on the swing, or will always take the best roles in whatever make-believe game is going on. I'll often be in the house and hear all of this. When it is the other girls, I barely notice. It is just kids being kids.

But when I hear Bailey or Rachel, my girls, acting that way, I immediately bristle. I have different expectations for them. We've talked at length with them about the fact that Elizabeth and I don't care so much if they are the smartest or fastest or prettiest girls in their classes, but we care very much that they be kind to others, that they share, that they not leave any one out or pick on anyone. So, when I hear them doing just that, I feel (there's no other way to say it) *wrath.*

Do you see a contrast here between my response and the judge's? His was solely due to the law; that was his concern. There was nothing personal in his judgment. In fact, that was the point. In my case, the opposite was true. It was precisely *because* of my relationship to Bailey and Rachel that their behavior caused me anger. Their mean or selfish play was not just hurtful to the other kids involved; it was an affront to the kind of family we want ours to be, the way we want to live as a family in the world as followers of Jesus. Their relationships to our family created a different level of expectations for all of their relationships, and that was the problem.

Which of these kinds of wrathful justice best describes God? We have already looked at the forming of God's specific relationship with Abraham in the cutting of a covenant with him. That story, in Genesis 15, makes it very clear that it is relationship God is after and that God is willing to bear the weight of maintaining that relationship because Abraham cannot. Four hundred and thirty years later, God again moves powerfully to sustain this relationship with Abraham's family, now grown to be the millions of Israelites enslaved in Egypt. He acts powerfully to rescue them.

After this, God takes them to Mount Sinai, where Moses climbs the mountain and God gives him the Law (think Charlton Heston in *The Ten Commandments* if you are old enough to remember that movie). Quite a large portion of four books of the Old Testament (Exodus, Leviticus, Numbers, and Deuteronomy) are devoted to the details of this Law and, due to the sheer volume of it, it is easy to get the sense that God cares more about us keeping rules than anything else. It is easy to believe that he's a whole lot like the judge in Dixon, Illinois.

In fact, in addition to all of these rules, God gives the Israelites a series of actions they can take when they break the rules. They are given sacrifices to offer. Sacrifices were commonplace in the religions of the ancient world. One never knew what the gods might do—when it would rain and when it wouldn't, when the crops would thrive and when they'd wither. People viewed themselves as being at the whim of their gods, and sacrifices were seen as a way to try to get the gods on your side. "If we feed them, perhaps they'll be happy with us." If the gods were fed something precious, perhaps they'd be happier still. In this kind of world, it's not hard to see where human sacrifice is not so much barbaric as just trying to offer the gods the most precious thing we have because they demand to be fed.

Is that what Israel's God is like? Is that what the Law and the sacrifices of the Old Testament are about? Is it possible that, though sacrifices in the Old Testament look on the surface just like the "feeding the hungry and angry god" sacrifices of other religions, a very different dynamic is at work? Is the Old Testament God a distant God who will be good to us only if we can jump over the bar of this massive law and offer good enough sacrifices when we don't? The important things to keep in mind here are that Israel has *already been in a relationship with God for 430 years* before they get the law and that God has *just rescued them* when they were *utterly helpless* slaves in Egypt. The whole point of God passing through the animals with Abraham and God's deliverance of the Israelites in Egypt is that God *knows* we are utterly helpless and yet desires to relate with us anyway. A God who does those things does not seem to fit with the angry, unpredictable, and hungry gods of the rest of the ancient world.

This is the choice we're faced with. Does God give Israel the law and the sacrifices to say, "If you keep these, I'll be willing to be in relationship with you," or "I have put you into a relationship with me. These laws are the shape of what that relationship looks like, and these sacrifices will help you remain in it?" Are the sacrifices Israel's gift to make happy the angry God, or are they the gift of the loving God to the people God desires to be in restored relationship with?

If the choice is the latter (that the law and the sacrifices were a gift from a loving, relating God to a people already in relationship with God), then justice and God's wrath take on a whole new tone. They begin to look a lot more like my being frustrated that my daughters are not always kind and inclusive in their play, not because they've transgressed an abstract legal code, but because I love them and their behavior does damage to who we are as a family.

Often, when Christians are talking about God and justice, we tend toward one of two extremes. Either God is concerned with justice in the traffic court judge's sense and has no choice but to throw the book at us because justice requires it, or God is loving and so can never be angry with us. I believe that placing God's wrath in the framework of relationships, the relationships between a loving parent and that parent's children, for example, allows both God's love and God's justice to not contradict one another. They aren't even two ideas that God somehow has to hold in balance or tension. God is angry with our sinful behavior *because* God first loves us. If I had no concern at all for how my daughters acted, one could question whether I really loved them at all.

Does Revenge Have the Power to Heal?

Or Would God Punish a Handful of Grain?

I N 1994, SOUTH AFRICA elected Nelson Mandela as its president. This was not just any person being elected president of just any country. This was a black man being elected the president of a country that had months previously been in its fourth decade of state-mandated apartheid, or separateness. In 1948, South Africa had formalized and intensified policies that had loosely been in place since the 1800s. Apartheid took away the right of black South Africans to be citizens in their own country. It limited their movements. It greatly curtailed their opportunities to be educated, hold most jobs, and own property. Essentially, it made them prisoners in their own country. It concentrated power in the hands of Afrikaners, white South Africans of Dutch descent, and other white Europeans. During the decades of formal apartheid, thousands of black South Africans were unjustly imprisoned, tortured, or killed by government security forces.

As apartheid ended in 1994, many braced for retribution from black South Africans. Having suffered economically and physically at the hands of white South Africa, many assumed the nation would now enter another era of violence. Payback time.

It did not happen.

How was this possible? Many things were at play, and the road forward has certainly not been easy, but most point to two men and one event as the keys. President Mandela, who himself had spent many years in South African prisons, and Archbishop Desmond Tutu, the Christian leader for much of black South Africa, led an effort to establish the Truth and Reconciliation Commission. In his book, *No Future Without Forgiveness*, Tutu says that he and others felt that the options most expected of them, to either seek retribution (in mob violence or in an organized manner like the Nuremburg Trials of Nazi criminals after World War II), or "let bygones be bygones . . . [an approach] sought after by the members of the previous government and those who had carried out their behest in the security forces."[1] The new leadership sought a different way. Tutu

---

1. Tutu, *No Future Without Forgiveness*, 24.

describes it as a way driven not by *retributive justice* (payback) but by an African tribal concept of *ubuntu,* which could lead to the "the healing of breaches."[2] This is the idea of *restorative justice,* with an emphasis upon the healing of broken relationships through reconciliation. *Ubuntu,* which Tutu stresses is very difficult to translate to Western language or thought categories, means one is "generous, you are hospitable, you are friendly and caring and compassionate. You share what you have. It is to say, 'My humanity is caught up, is inextricably bound up, in yours.'"[3] Or, as a Zulu maxim puts it, "A person is a person through other people."

This was not a justice without consequence, which would be no justice at all. The wrong done had to be named and owned by the guilty. They had to look their victims in the eye and confess their deeds. This was also not vindictive punishment. Out of this quest for *ubuntu* came the Truth and Reconciliation Commission. Essentially, the Commission held out the prospect of amnesty for those who had committed criminal acts under state-sponsored apartheid. To receive amnesty, however, members of the government or the security forces had to come before the Commission *and* those whom they'd wounded (either the victims themselves or their relatives) and openly confess what they had done. These confessions would be recorded, remembered in a very tangible way, but then forgiveness, amnesty, even a sort of forgetfulness would be offered. While many did not receive amnesty because they were deemed to have been dishonest about their actions, almost one thousand Afrikaners received amnesty from the Commission.

While the Commission has not brought society-wide *ubuntu* in South Africa, the world has been amazed that, given its violent and systematically unjust history, the transition out of apartheid has been remarkably peaceful. I believe one can argue that Mandela and Tutu were right: Restorative justice has provided a better way forward than retributive justice.

In fact, and here is where we return to the previous discussion of the sacrifices in the Bible, one might ask if retributive justice ever really *works* at all. Huh? Don't the wronged have their right to be avenged? How can I even suggest that parents who have seen their small child violently murdered not demand the death penalty for the murderer?

2. Ibid., 54.
3. Ibid., 55.

I think, on many levels, this urge for retribution is common to us all. In fact, at times, we ache for this kind of justice. "You'll pay for this!" I am not questioning this desire or that it feels fair, right, and reasonable.

I *am* questioning one thing about it, however. Is it even possible? Not is it reasonable to want, but does it work? Do the loved ones of the victim actually find peace in the punishment or death of the perpetrator? While it is argued that the perpetrator must be "made to pay" for the wrong in order to restore the dignity of the victim, is this really the only way to restore dignity? Does not Jesus' injunction to "turn the other cheek" or the success of nonviolent resistance movements lead by Mohandas Gandhi and Martin Luther King argue that dignity can be maintained without retribution? In the cases of Gandhi's work in South Africa and India and King's Civil Rights Movement in the United States, at the heart of the decision to pursue change peacefully was a decision *not* to seek retribution upon those who had perpetuated great wrong.

Can retributive or proportional justice succeed? Even if the life of a murderer is taken, can the family of the victim feel that they have been adequately paid? Does it assuage the pain in any real way? Why do many family members talk of wrestling with anger, hate, and pain long after the execution that promised to bring closure? I imagine that there may be some sense of satisfaction, but compared to the ocean of loss, how does that measure up? What would be adequate retribution for the Holocaust?

Given the persistent, if not constant, rebellion of Israel and all of humanity toward God, how would the blood of an animal equal their guilt? How could that blood *satisfy*? How much blood would be enough?

I would like to suggest that the blood sacrifices in the Bible did *not* serve to give God revenge for wrongs done, but instead were a means by which God offered to heal and restore us. I think the overarching story of God as told by the Bible already suggests this, but there is a rather obscure little verse in the heart of the establishment of the sacrifices themselves that I believe helps strongly make the point. It's easy to miss, however, and in fact, until pointed out to me a couple of years ago, I'd read the Bible for years without even noticing or thinking about it.

In Leviticus 5, God sets out for Israel the procedures for the sacrifice of *atonement*. This is the sacrifice that most symbolized the forgiveness or removal of sin from the people and their reconciliation to God. Early in the chapter, the individual is instructed to bring a sheep or goat, the best that they had. At this point, the idea that God wants blood as payback or revenge still might make sense. Maybe God does want to punish this sheep, and its owner, for the sin of the individual. The instructions don't end there, however. If the person bringing the sacrifice could not afford a lamb or goat, two doves would do. But, still, it doesn't stop there. If the person is truly poor and cannot even afford two doves, a handful of grain would do.

How does one punish or pour out one's wrath on a handful of grain? If what God is after is blood to pay for guilt, how can a few kernels of grain possibly do the job?

Doesn't it seem like the main issue here is for the person to genuinely and sincerely come before God and name his or her sin, just like in the Truth and Reconciliation Commission in South Africa, and for God to provide a way for that person to be cleansed and to know, in a tangible way, that the sin has been removed?

One of the ways blood was viewed in the Bible, as well as in other religions around the world, is as a cleansing or purifying agent. In that sense, it is not that the death of the animal was demanded as punishment for the sin, but that the blood actually represented a healing or life-giving cleansing. Growing up as a boy in a church that sang old hymns a lot, I often sang the words, "What can wash away my sin? Nothing but the blood of Jesus. What can make me whole again? Nothing but the blood of Jesus." This view of sacrificial blood as something that washes and cleans, rather than represents vengeance, is what this song was talking about: Blood as a "gift to cleanse you," not as "a price to satisfy my rage."

What about "an eye for an eye and a tooth for a tooth?"

But, you may ask, doesn't the Bible itself call on us to exact proportional retribution? In the Old Testament, aren't the Israelites told to take "an eye for an eye (lost) and a tooth for a tooth (knocked out)?" On the surface, it certainly appears so.

A look at the context of the times, however, suggests a somewhat different understanding. The world in which the Old Testament events play out was not a world ruled by scrupulously crafted and followed laws. It was, largely, a world of ever escalating violence. If I wronged you, you would kill me. If you killed me, my relatives would kill you and your entire family. Your village or clan would respond by wiping out my entire village, and so on and so on.

Viewed in this light, the admonition to "take an eye for an eye and a tooth for a tooth" looks infinitely less like God-sanctioned violence and revenge and more like God working to control and limit revenge, retribution, and the cycle of human violence.

Two Words: *Hesed* and *Emmanuel*

W HAT'S IN A WORD? Sometimes, almost everything. Two words from the Bible go far in summing up the entire story of who God is and what in the world is going on in all of the Bible's story. In doing so, they sum up our story as well. The words? *Hesed* and *Emmanuel*. One word gets translated into less precise words in all of our English Bibles and so therefore needs to be pointed out. The other does get translated well but appears only once, and still is of utmost importance.

HESED

Hesed is a Hebrew word, an Old Testament word. As is often the case with language, translating a word from one language—moving it from its home, the context and story in which it was born, into another language—is difficult to do. Such is the case with *hesed*. In English Bibles, it shows up as "steadfast love," "loving kindness," "mercy," or "love." In each case, the English version feels two dimensional compared to the three-dimensional richness of the Hebrew word.

Hesed is a word best translated into stories and illustrations. God's sparing the life of Cain after he murders his brother Abel is *hesed*. God's passing through the animals on Abraham's behalf in their covenant ceremony is *hesed*. God's giving a child to ninety-year-old Sarah, Abraham's wife, is *hesed*. God's actions of deliverance toward Israel enslaved in Egypt are *hesed*. God's relationship with David, the Godly king who also commits murder and adultery, is *hesed*. In fact, the Psalms—poems, many of which were written by David—is the place where *hesed* appears most in the Old Testament. God's mercy upon sinful Nineveh that so infuriated Jonah is *hesed*. Hosea's love for his adulterous wife Gomer is *hesed*. God's deliverance of the Jews from exile in Babylon is *hesed*.

In short, the entire Old Testament could be summed up with this basic plotline: humans (first Adam and Eve, then Abraham, and finally, the people of Israel) are offered relationship with God; humanity rejects God; God extends *hesed* to them and restores them. When the Bible says, "God is love," what it really means is "God is *hesed*." God's love is not a love that is deserved, earned, or shared between equals. Philosophers sometimes talk about asymmetrical relationships, relationships where there is not a sense of "you scratch my back and I'll scratch yours; you love me and I'll love you," but where I am called upon to love regardless of the other's qualifications or response. God's *hesed* toward us is something like that, only it is not required. It is just offered.

It might be tempting at this point to cry out, "Wait a minute. That's only half the picture! What about the God who is Holy? The God who demands justice?" That is a very fair question. I don't believe saying that God is fundamentally, at the very core, *hesed* is to deny that God is also Holy. Mercy doesn't wash sin under the rug. It doesn't pretend sin is not there. A Bible dictionary from the nineteenth century says that mercy is "compassion toward the helpless, the miserable." Mercy doesn't say, "Sin? What sin? I don't see any problem here." It says, "You are helpless; let me help you. You are without hope; let me give you hope. You are utterly unworthy of love; let me love you."

EMMANUEL

When the angel tells utterly freaked-out Joseph that his fiancé, Mary, is pregnant, not because she has been cheating on him but by a miracle of God, the Gospel of Matthew adds the tagline, "All this took place to fulfill what the Lord had said to the prophet Isaiah; 'The virgin will conceive and give birth to a son and they will call him *Emmanuel*, which means *God with us.*'"[1] I suspect that for a lot of us, reading those words conjures up some Christmas TV show or another with stirring music and glorious light. It's a beautiful phrase, *Emmanuel: God with us.* We recite it once a year and move on, not giving it another thought.

It's very typical to say that God's great act of love toward humanity is Jesus' death on the cross. It certainly is a mind-boggling thing that God would do that. I'd propose, however, that at least as significant as the death of Jesus is his birth. The death on the cross is a great sacrifice, but think about the birth. The infinite, transcendent, limitless God pouring all of God's self into a helpless, very finite, profoundly limited human body, a helpless baby. Theologians talk about *kenosis*, God's "emptying." When they do, they are talking a little bit about the cross, but they are mostly talking about the birth. Either that or the incarnation—God choosing not

---

1. Matthew 1:22–23.

to be everything and everywhere at once but to be right here, in flesh that could be touched.

Why, *Emmanuel*? Jesus is *Emmanuel* because of *hesed*. God's love is not a love that can stay at a distance. It is not a love that can sit and watch and think, "I sure hope they get it right down there." God's love is a love that enters in. Always. From the creation, to the Exodus and the Tabernacle, from the birth of a baby to the death on a cross, God's love enters in, identifies with, is present with and for us.

A very simplistic but also profound summary of Christianity (and in a real way, Judaism) in relation to all the other religions of the world is this: All religions can be described as humanity climbing its way to God (meditating enough, being reincarnated enough, denying self enough). Christianity is God coming down to us. There are certainly more nuances to it than that, but it's a pretty fair description. Other religions don't have *hesed* or *Emmanuel*. They have a love given when it is earned. They offer a God, gods, or Nirvana that waits for us to find our way there. Christianity has a God who sees our helplessness, acts in merciful and relentless love, and enters in.

Hesed and *Emmanuel*.

What Does It Look Like When God-with-Us
Shows Up?

OKAY, SO GOD SHOWS up in your neighborhood. What would God do? Who would God talk to? What kind of things would God do? The Gospels are our best glimpse at what that would look like. If we really believe Jesus is God in the flesh, God-with-us, then how Jesus acts shows us who God is and what God feels. Two healing miracles from the Gospels give us a glimpse.

In the first, Jesus and a large crowd of people are walking along when a leper calls out to them. In our world, leprosy is extremely rare. A degenerative nerve disease, it has largely been eradicated around the world. In Jesus' time, this was not the case. Not only was leprosy common, it was feared. Lepers in Jesus' days were *unclean*. This meant that observant Jews could not have any physical contact with them without becoming ceremonially contaminated themselves. While there were many ways to be unclean, leprosy is the example most often seen in the Gospels.

A leper would literally be an outcast from his or her community. Lepers could not live in towns with others; they survived the best they could in caves or the wilderness. They could not be with their families and friends. They could not be touched. If they came into a town, looking for food, for example, they had to yell out, "Leper! Unclean!" so that people would have warning to get out of the way and hide. As devastating as leprosy was to one's body, it was also devastating to the soul. It was a sentence to a life of utter isolation.

The leper in this story, found in three of the four Gospels, calls out to Jesus, "Lord, if you are willing, you can make me clean." Jesus replies, "I am willing." And then he reaches out and touches him and the leprosy is gone. End of story. The Gospels move on to the next scene.

I'd like to linger for a moment. There was a subtle moment there that I think most of us miss that is profoundly significant. Did you catch it? What is the one thing an observant Jew cannot, under any circumstances do? *Touch* a leper. Jesus reaches out and *touches* him.

The leper's body was being ravaged by leprosy. Jesus addressed that. The leper was also a person, a human being, created for relationship, who lived his life in complete absence of relationship. As serious as the damage was to his body, so was the carnage of his soul. Jesus also addresses that. He reaches out and *touches* him. He did not have to do that. He could have healed him from a distance. He could have remained apart, saying, "Bless you, be healed, but I'm pretty busy and need to keep going." Instead, he stopped and touched him. This is what God-with-us looks like.

Another scene takes place on the way to Jairus's house. Again, this story appears in multiple Gospels, though Mark's version gives the most details. It is a big deal that Jesus is on the way to Jairus's house, because Jairus is a big deal. He is the leader of the local synagogue and a public figure in town. He's an important figure, and his daughter is gravely ill. He has begged Jesus to come and heal her, and Jesus has agreed.

The crowd is on the move, no doubt getting bigger as it winds through the narrow streets of town. I am sure that the disciples, Jesus' closest followers, are very excited. I mean, this is a *great* career move. Healing Jairus's daughter is going to get Jesus noticed. If this event took place today, it certainly would mean a spot on the evening news. Who knows, maybe CNN would pick up the story!

All of a sudden, everything comes crashing to a stop. In the middle of the narrow, crowded road, with an excited, urgently moving crowd, Jesus has stopped walking. In fact, he seems to be talking to someone.

A woman has snuck up to Jesus in the crowd and touched him. Actually, she just touched his clothes, but somehow Jesus has noticed it and has stopped to talk to her. Who is this woman, and what is going on?

Mark tells us that she was a woman with hemorrhages, bleeding, that had lasted for twelve years. Bleeding like this in Jewish society would have made her, just like the leper, *unclean*. Twelve years of isolation and physical suffering. But that is not all. Mark also says that she had "suffered under many physicians and had spent all she had, but rather than getting better had gotten worse."[1] For twelve years, she has been ill, alone, and increasingly destitute financially. How do we know all this?

Because, when Jesus asks, "Who touched me?" she came forward and "told him the whole truth."[2] In other words, she told Jesus the whole story. All twelve years of it. "I haven't had a soul to talk to and to listen to me in twelve years, and you don't know how awful it's been."

1. Mark 5:26.
2. Mark 5:33.

When is this happening, this Jesus standing and patiently listening to every word of this lonely woman on the social fringe? It is happening on the way to the Big Event. It is happening as everyone—Jairus, the disciples, and the crowd—is in a hurry to get to the show. You can even see that in the response of the disciples in verse 31, "You see the crowd pressing in on you; how can you say, 'Who touched me?'" Their impatience leaps off the page. "Come on, Jesus! Sure, she's healed. That's great, but we've got places to get to. *Important* people to heal. What are you doing listening to this homeless beggar going on and on and on?!"

Well, this is God-with-us, after all. We are not just seeing some magic man or miracle worker. As Jesus stands and listens, as if there is nowhere else in the world he needs to be at that moment other than listening to this woman, we are seeing the heart of God played out before our eyes.

(In case you are unfamiliar with the ending, Jesus gets to Jairus's house and heals his daughter, too. Jesus doesn't care *just* for people no one else notices or cares about. Everyone is worthy of notice, even the rich and the powerful.)

What Parents Do

Now, some of us have less than ideal parents. Some of us have experienced abandonment from our parents, physically or emotionally. Some of us have been battered by our parents in many and various ways. I don't question that many of us have negative pictures in our minds of parents or parenting. I do think, however, that the reality that bad parenting is so painful hints at the fact that parenting could and should be so much more. Sometimes it is. I'd like to look at a couple of moments where human parents help illustrate some of who God is as our heavenly parent.

At the 1992 Summer Olympics in Barcelona, Spain, Derek Redmond was entered in the four-hundred-meter dash representing Great Britain. In his semifinal heat, he needed to finish in the top four to advance to the final. With less than two hundred meters to go, he was in a great position to earn a spot in the Olympic final. Then his right hamstring popped. He dropped to the track in agony and sat there for a few tortured moments. And then he got up.

To the amazement of the crowd in the stadium and millions watching around the world on television, Derek Redmond was going to try to finish his race, on one leg. He began to hop around the turn, unable to put even the slightest weight on his right leg.

Suddenly, into the TV screen came a middle-aged man in shorts and a t-shirt. He had pushed past security guards, jumped the railing separating spectators from the track, and was running toward Redmond. When he reached him, he came alongside him and took his right arm and supported Redmond as he hopped along.

This was Derek's dad. He had come to the Olympics to watch his son's proudest athletic moment. He had a ticket to sit up in the stands. As this proud moment turned into one of anguish and pain, however, Derek's dad was not content to sit and watch; he had to enter in on behalf of his son. He had to come alongside. His presence on the track didn't change the outcome of the race. Thomas still failed to make the final, finishing minutes after the other competitors. He still faced the pain and agony of a long recovery from a massive injury. But, in that moment on the track, he was not alone. In his greatest moment of anguish, his father refused to allow him to experience it alone and raced to his side.

You may not know the name Dick Hoyt, but if you've ever poked around YouTube or been to a banquet that featured a motivational talk, there's a good chance you've heard his story. Dick Hoyt has a profoundly disabled son named Rick. Rick cannot walk or use most of his muscles; he can speak only through typing with the one tortured hand he has use of.

Years ago, Rick heard of a 5K road race to benefit a young person in his community. He typed to his dad that he wanted to do the race. Obviously, Rick could not do it on his own, but his dad could push him. So, he did.

That began what has become Team Hoyt, a cottage industry in motivational talks and videos. Father and son have now completed dozens of 26.2-mile marathons and even several Ironman triathlons. Rick, the son, has never taken a step in his life, let alone entered and finished a race. Every inch of every race is covered by the efforts of his father. When the triathlon is in the water, Dick pulls his son on a raft while he swims. When they enter the bike phase, Rick rides on a seat affixed to Dick's bike. In the last running phase, a full 26.2-mile marathon in an Ironman, Dick pushes Rick every inch of the way. Dick does for his son what Rick cannot do for himself.

God is a God who enters in. God is a God who "tabernacles" with. God is Emmanuel, God with us. God is a God who does for us—bearing the weight of our sin and moving toward us in reconciliation—what we could not do ourselves.

Are You Hungry?

THE TWENTIETH-CENTURY BRITISH CHRISTIAN C. S. Lewis said that just because we are hungry doesn't mean we will find food. He went on to argue, however, that being hungry does mean that we are creatures who were made to eat.

We hunger for all kinds of things other than food. Two of the most significant are love and home.

What does this say about who we are and what we were made for?

PART FOUR

God Putting All Things Right

O NE OF MY FAVORITE *pieces of classical music (actually, one of the only pieces I'm really that familiar with) is Aaron Copeland's "Appalachian Spring." My Dad had a cassette of it (I'm that old), and we listened to it often while making trips cross-country to visit relatives when I was young. One of the great things that Copeland does (and this appears in other compositions by other composers, too) is that early on he introduces a hint of a melody line. Sometimes there is just a phrase, sometimes more, usually played by a minor or quiet instrument. And then it's gone, but before long it comes back again. This time it is a little different but recognizable as the same melody, the same theme. Building. Circling. And then, finally, it bursts to the fore, the entire orchestra now robustly and joyously swelling with the famous Shaker melody, "A Gift to be Simple."*

That is how the narrative of God told in the Bible works. Shalom, hesed, covenant, *and* tabernacle *all appear throughout and then momentarily get swallowed up by the seemingly unrelenting story of human weakness and sin. But they are never gone for very long. Out again come hints of this God who loves, who is present with, who will not relent in mercy.*

Now, in this next part, the entire orchestra takes up the theme. Jesus has come. This is the point to which the entire story has built, around which it has circled. What follows are pieces dealing with this glorious reality. All that was hinted at and promised is now here.

In the introduction, I said this was a book about the cross of Jesus, about what the cross means. And yet, so far I haven't said much specifically about the cross. What we've been doing is sort of like this: Imagine you are climbing a huge mountain. Where I live, in the Pacific Northwest, there are many massive, dormant volcanoes in the region. The nearest to my home is Mount Hood, which rises from sea level just east of Portland, Oregon, to more than eleven thousand feet at its summit. If you were to climb Mount Hood, you would not be advised to head straight up its slopes. They're too steep. You would circle, switch back, and gradually move higher but do so in a way that at times seemed like you were not making direct progress. That's what I've been trying to do here. We have been moving around topics that are central to Jesus and the cross: relationality, the nature of God and how God has acted in history, human brokenness. All the while, we have been moving ever closer to the summit. And now we are here. But, before we get to the peak, I'd like to ask your indulgence in one more mental exercise. I will make one quick detour into philosophy, and then on to the main event.

St. John's Cross, Iona, 2007

An Exercise in Perspective

MOUNT HOOD LOOMS AS a dominant feature on the horizon for large portions of Oregon and southern Washington. Some people see it virtually every day of the year. A colleague of mine lives in East Portland on a big hill and has an unobstructed view of the west face of Mount Hood from his living room window. Irv could easily sit on his porch and draw sketches of the mountain. Depending upon the time of day, the light on the mountain would change and the amount of snow would vary from winter to summer, but the physical mountain that he sees looks the same day after day.

When one flies into the Portland airport from the east, Mount Hood looms for several minutes just out of the left window, seemingly close enough to touch. An artistically inclined passenger could whip out a sketch pad and draw a picture of Hood's north face. If that passenger were a frequent flier, she could produce picture after picture, flight after flight. Someone living in the high desert town of Maupin, Oregon, due east of Hood, could do the same, producing pictures of the mountain's east face. A climber atop one of the Three Sisters peaks to Hood's south could produce works of its south face.

Imagine that I invite all four artists over for coffee because I really want to know what Mount Hood looks like. I tell them, "Okay, which of you has a drawing that tells me what the mountain *really* looks like?" All present their drawings, each arguing that his or hers is the true representation. "Hey, I've looked at this mountain one hundred times and drawn it that many. I can say with certainty that this is the mountain. My drawing is true." Each is convincing. What am I to do? Who am I to believe?

The problem when it comes to drawing Mount Hood is clear. All perspectives are right and all are wrong. The reality is that Mount Hood is so vast that no one vantage point can capture all of it. Each artist could faithfully render the view from his or her location, but they are completely unable to see the other perspectives, so each drawing is both accurate yet hopelessly incomplete.

All approaches to understanding the cross of Jesus, to explaining it in a theory or an illustration, are going to be guilty of the same thing. Each approach may very well accurately describe one aspect of what the cross means, but the event, the reality is so vast that in capturing one facet, any theory is guaranteed to miss much of what is really going on. This is true of my perspective as well.

So what are we to do? There are a few options. One is to fight about it, and the person who argues loudest and longest and is able to intellectually bully the rest wins. Perhaps my friend Irv would be able to argue the other Hood artists into submission and convince me that he alone is right.

A second option would be to give up. How can we have any idea of what we're talking about when each perspective is different? Let's just say, "Everyone thinks what they think, sees what they see, and we cannot have any idea of what is really true. It's all relative."

A third option would be to reject each of the first two and say, "I recognize that my picture is only part of the view, but it's a good picture and it's important if we want to get at the whole thing. Why don't we take the insights of each of our perspectives and put them together. In that way, we'll all contribute to understanding the whole that is bigger than what we can see by ourselves."

The advantage of multiple perspectives is at least twofold. On the one hand, having a different perspective can verify what my view suspects but can't be sure of. "Look, your drawing ends right where mine picks up, and they really seem to fit together." On the other hand, other perspectives can be helpful correctives if I'm getting something totally wrong. If Irv, my friend to the west of Mount Hood, were to draw Hood with an even larger mountain looming just behind it, the other artists could quickly point out that this is a mistake. Mount Hood, in fact, stands alone in terms of any mountains for many, many miles around.

Many people see only option one or option two when talking about theology or the things of God. It's all or nothing. Either someone is right and everyone else is wrong, or truth is totally up for grabs. I feel profoundly uncomfortable with both of those options. In moving now to talk specifically about the cross, I'm giving the perspective of the cross that I see from where I sit. I think there are some very good reasons to believe that there's a great deal of truth to it. I also recognize that it doesn't encompass every issue at hand and is, therefore, incomplete and in need of other perspectives.

The Center Point of Human History

ONE NEED NOT BE a follower of Jesus to recognize that, at least in terms of sheer volume of pages, no life and death in human history has captivated the minds of men and women for the last two thousands years like that of Jesus. There is simply no one to compare him with. While the teachings of Mohammed or the Buddha certainly have drawn millions by their power and beauty, the lives of these teachers are often mysteries to us, and they remain relatively unexamined.

This is not so with Jesus. His birth and death, in particular, have been rendered by thousands upon thousands of works of art. Poems and songs have been composed. Book after book has been written trying to come to terms with, to make sense of this man, this life, this death. Even religious traditions other than Christianity claim him as a wise man or prophet in their view of the world. Tragically, churches have been split, wars fought, and individuals killed over disagreements about this or that point in who and what Jesus was.

Given that, is there anything that can be said confidently about Jesus? What follows are a few things that even divergent traditions within Christianity have held to be true for more than two thousand years.

- Jesus' birth was miraculous and represented, in a real way, God entering into the human condition in a particular human person. (Some believe that Jesus' mother, Mary, was perpetually a virgin and others do not, but orthodox Christianity has consistently affirmed that Jesus' conception was miraculous.)

- Jesus lived a life of exemplary purity and profound teaching. Even those outside of Christianity find his teaching to be of immense wisdom. Gandhi's vision of nonviolence as a means for social transformation arose, to a great degree, from his reading of the Sermon on the Mount.

- Jesus attracted the devotion of many but also drew the opposition of large portions of those holding religious and political power in his day.

- Jesus' teaching and ministry seems to have been particularly good news for those in need. The poor, the outcast, the sick, the socially marginalized (i.e., prostitutes, tax collectors, women in general, and Samaritans) seemed to be drawn to him.

- Jesus' comments indicate that he, in some way, saw himself as being sent by God to particularly fulfill the story of Israel, to come to their aid or to remove that which oppressed them, and to forgive sins.

- Though innocent, Jesus was arrested, put through a sham of a trial by both religious and political leaders (Jewish and Roman), and sentenced to die.

- Though expressing that he had the power to bring about his deliverance at any point, Jesus allowed himself to be crucified.

- Three days later, Jesus rose from the dead. (Some who claim to be Christians deny an actual physical resurrection. For two millennia, however, Christians have held the actual resurrection as central to Christian faith.) Immediately after his death, Jesus' followers began to exclaim that he had risen, a claim that in its early voicing could have been refuted easily by either the Jewish leaders or the Romans. They only needed to produce the body.

- Within a very short time, Jesus' followers began to believe and tell others that Jesus' coming to earth and his death and resurrection were the central events in human history. They came to believe that everything was changed by these events.

- For those of us tempted to say, "I don't really like all this gory talk about crosses and death. I'd rather focus upon Jesus' teaching and ministry," I'd say this: The Bible contains four accounts of Jesus' life. While each offers its own unique perspective on Jesus and what he did (and the teaching and ministry of Jesus is certainly *very* important), each Gospel devotes more words and pages to the death and resurrection of Jesus than any other event. To each of the Gospel writers, Jesus' death and resurrection took on a significance that outweighed even the greatest of Jesus' teaching or acts of mercy.

- Jesus died as our substitute. Some may read that and quickly disagree. "Substitution" often gets used exclusively in terms of a particular view of the cross: the idea that Jesus died as our substitute in terms of receiving our punishment in the court of God's righteous judgment. Some find this idea, that *substitution* means God angrily punishing his own innocent son, to be difficult to stomach. A wise professor once argued that this understanding of the term was too limiting. "Any view of the cross that says that Jesus does something on the cross for humanity that humanity could not do for itself is substitutionary." I agree with that. In that sense, while disagreeing at times about particulars, Christians throughout history have viewed the cross as Jesus doing something there for us that we could not do for ourselves. I would suggest, though, that those who feel they alone have the true understanding of "substitutionary atonement" should expand their view to include other perspectives. Likewise, just because they seek to avoid some of the excesses they perceive in "penal substitution," others should still robustly embrace the "substitutionary" elements of all of the biblical metaphors used to describe what Jesus accomplishes on the cross.

Some claiming common ground with the Christian tradition deny part or most of the above list, while others see no need for any kind of atonement at all. Looking at two thousand years of Church thinking as a whole, I am choosing to say that those who see no need for Jesus to provide atonement for us are outside of what it has traditionally meant by "being a Christian." That is not to say those who question any of that are unequivocally outside of Christianity in all respects, just that in terms of this important Christian doctrine, their beliefs are outside of the mainstream of Christian belief.

While putting forward some things that Christians agree about, I've opened the door to all kinds of things about which there has been much less agreement. The following are examples:

How was Jesus conceived?

Did Mary ever sin?

How much do Jesus' teachings matter? Are they as important as his death and resurrection? Are they more important than his death or significantly less so?

What did Jesus save us from? From God? From Satan? From ourselves?

How?

Is our problem that we are guilty? Enslaved? Sick? Misguided? Some combination?

Who was this salvation for? Everyone? Only those God chooses? Only those who choose God? Only those who choose God in a certain and very particular way?

Once saved, what are we supposed to do next? Does it matter?

I am not going to begin to try to answer every one of those questions. For one thing, I'm not nearly smart enough to have a definitive answer for many of them. For another, for every answer I could give, numerous other serious and thoughtful Christians throughout history have answered them differently.

I *am* going to do this. I am going to contend that in some way, Jesus' death on the cross and resurrection from the dead deals with the sin of humanity in a comprehensive and final way. While exactly how this is accomplished may be the most mysterious and *beyond-nailed-down-perfect* understanding of any doctrine in the Christian faith, I think that the story of the Bible in general and a couple of specific stories of the Bible in particular give us clear hints or clear, if still open-ended, frameworks to think about this issue. For example, we've already looked at the *tabernacling* nature of God in the Old Testament. This is the idea that God seems, over and over again, to be a God who enters into the human situation, into our joys and sufferings. It is the idea that God is a God who is not distant, but rather a God who gets involved. Also, attention has been drawn to the story of the Exodus, that God is a God who hears our cries and sets about to rescue us. We've seen that behind this entering in and rescuing nature of God lies a God who relates and that to be human is to be relational. We've also seen how, over and over again, God acts graciously in situations where humans are helpless or barren. God's grace does not supplement our human effort, but God particularly helps those who are helpless. These realities, shown in the stories of God in the Bible, certainly give us frameworks to help us make sense of Jesus.

Now we turn to two particular stories, each told by God in uniquely specific ways that, to me, give us clues as to God's intention in the life and work of Jesus.

Life as Parable: Hosea and Gomer

THE OLD TESTAMENT PROPHETS spoke for God. Sometimes coming with a message of comfort, more often coming with pleading and warning, the prophets were sent to get God's message across to the people of Israel. Usually, their words were the central part of their message. In fact, for many of them, we don't know much about who they were or what they did. For some, however, their actions were a central part of their message. No prophet characterizes this more than Hosea, who lived about seven hundred years before Jesus.

Hosea lived in a time when Israel had largely turned away from God. Idol worship and abuse of the poor and weak were the rule of the day. God comes to Hosea with a stunningly odd request. God asks him to marry a promiscuous woman. Some translations even say that he is to marry a prostitute. What?! Isn't this a God who values marital purity? Why in the world would God ask a holy man, a prophet, to do such a thing?

The rest of the sentence gives the answer. "Go marry a promiscuous woman and have children with her *for like an adulterous wife this land is guilty of unfaithfulness to the Lord.*"[1] God is setting up a drama here, and Hosea gets the starring role. Here's how the parts basically play out: "Hosea, you will be playing the part of me, God. How you relate to your wife will be how I relate to Israel. And your wife, Gomer, she will be playing the part of Israel [who, remember, plays the part of all of humanity in God's big drama]. How she loves you, or most of the time doesn't, will be how Israel relates to me."

So they get married and have a couple of kids. The Bible isn't clear as to whether Gomer was unfaithful from the very start or if she just became so after a time, but that really isn't the point. Before long, she is out sleeping around. Hosea is faced with a variety of options. He could divorce her. In his day and culture, he could have her stoned to death for committing adultery. Or he could continue to love her and pursue her. As he is acting out God's love for Israel in this relationship, he keeps on loving her. In fact, he comes up with a variety of plans to woo her back.

1. Hosea 1:2.

109

First, he sends their children to talk with her. Maybe seeing them will remind Gomer of what she's tossed away in chasing after these other lovers. This has no effect.

Next, he showers her with presents. He gives her silver and gold, new wines, and fine foods. He's not a rich man. Surely, she will see the extravagance of these gifts, recognize how much he loves her, and come home. But she doesn't. In fact, she takes the gifts and turns around and gives them to her lovers. She takes the gifts meant to woo her back to Hosea and uses them to drive a wedge even further between them.

Finally, he hits on a new plan. Perhaps he remembers back to the time when they first met and were courting—a time when things were better, before everything fell apart. "I'll take her out in the wilderness and speak tenderly to her. I will allure her," he thinks. Translation? "I know this great picnic spot out in the countryside. I'll take her there and read poetry to her, poetry I've written that will speak to her of my love." He gives this a try, but nothing comes of it.

The Bible again is not clear on the timing, but Gomer eventually ends up as a prostitute. Imagine the pain of this for Hosea. Their community is not large. How easy it would have been to be out running errands in town with their kids when they look up and see her working a street corner.

"Hey Dad, there's Mom! Let's go talk to her!"

"No. She's busy. Maybe some other time. Let's go."

In Hosea's culture, if one got so far in debt that there was no realistic way out, there was an option: selling oneself into slavery.

This is where Gomer ends up. She has walked away from the one who loved her truly, Hosea. She has slept with who knows how many men, some just for fun, some for money. Now she can't even get by doing that. She has decided to sell herself as a slave.

The day of the sale arrives. Again, this is not a big community, so everyone knows Hosea, and everyone knows Gomer. The sale likely takes place in the center of town. As Gomer climbs up on the slaver's block, so everyone can see her, evaluate her worth, and judge her, Hosea walks up.

The Bible is silent on what is going through the minds of the people in the crowd here, but I don't think it's hard to guess. As Hosea's friends watch him walk up, they most likely have one of two thoughts. Either, "Go home, you old fool. Haven't you been through enough humiliation because of Gomer? Just walk away and be done with her once and for all."

Or, "I didn't think he had it in him. For all these years he's kept on loving her, but now he's come his senses. He's come to watch her get what she deserves. He's come to watch her humiliation. Good for him."

The bidding starts. To everyone's surprise, Hosea raises his hand and makes a bid.

"I can't believe it! He's got more backbone than I thought. Finally, Hosea's out for a little revenge! He's going to buy her back and make her pay. She didn't want to be his wife; I wonder how she'll like being his slave. The humiliation and retribution will just go on and on! Way to go, Hosea!"

Why do I think that's what they are thinking? Because that's what I would think. Wouldn't you? We believe in love and second chances, to a point. But there comes a time, after enough hurt and betrayal, that love hardens to hate and all we want is payback. That's how we would respond to Gomer.

But remember, the point of this whole story is that Hosea is playing the part of God. He loves Gomer like God loves Israel. Like God loves us. "Love her as the Lord loves the Israelites,"[2] is the instruction Hosea has from God.

So he does. He buys her back. He pays for her in both money and grain, which signifies that he had to scrape together more than his bank account would hold to come up with enough.

The whole town has to have crowded around to see what the first interaction between Hosea and his whoring wife will be. Will he spit on her? Swear at her? Strike her? Gomer has to be thinking the same things. You can almost feel the fear she must be feeling as she cringes before him, waiting for the blow.

It never comes.

"You will call me 'my husband,'" Hosea says to Gomer, "You will no longer call me 'my master.'"

This is how God loves the Israelites. This is how God loves us. Being reconciled to his wife cost Hosea so much. It cost him most, if not all, of the wealth he had. That barely scratches the surface, though. It cost him his honor, his pride. He could have maintained all of that in the eyes of the community by rejecting his unfaithful wife, by walking away. To be reconciled with her, though, meant entering into her shame. From his at-

2. Hosea 1:2.

tempts to woo her back to his publicly purchasing her and declaring that she was not a slave but a wife, his actions took her shame and placed them upon himself.

Seven hundred years later, God would act out another, very similar drama. Only this time the cost would not be some money and some grain; it would be Jesus' life. The purchase wouldn't take place at a slaver's platform in the middle of town. It would happen on the cross.

Let Me Tell You Three Times,
Just in Case You Missed the Point

IN THE LATTER DAYS of his life, Jesus tells three remarkable stories that make much the same point as the story of Hosea and Gomer. They are collected together in Luke 15. Jesus tells these stories in response to religious leaders who were critical of him because he seemed so interested in spending time with people "good religious folks" don't spend time with—tax collectors and sinners. In these stories, Jesus explains to the religious leaders (and us) what he is about, what God is about.

The third of the three stories is the most famous, and we usually refer to it as "the parable of the prodigal son." When we tell it, it is a story of a foolish, rebellious son who leaves his dad, squanders his wealth, ruins his life, finally comes to his senses, and comes home, repentant and sorry. That telling misses the entire point of the story.

Let's back up for a moment. In Jewish culture, repeating something three times had special significance. To say something three times was to bind yourself to it. For example, getting a divorce was a simple process; all you had to do was say three times, "I divorce you." Triple repetition bound you to it.

Jesus tells three stories in Luke 15. Whatever the point of these stories is, Jesus is binding himself to their meaning.

The first story is a story about a shepherd and his sheep. It seems the shepherd has one hundred sheep out in the field and, sheep being the stupid animals that they are, one has wandered off and gotten lost. The shepherd faces a choice. He can either say, "I've still got ninety-nine sheep. That's pretty good," and head back home, or he can leave everything and search for the lost sheep. The shepherd searches for the lost sheep, and when he finds it, he is so excited that he throws a huge party for the whole neighborhood. (The neighbors must be thinking, "What's the big deal? A sheep is a sheep, but I'm not going to say no to a party!")

The second story makes the same point, just with minor character changes. This time it is a woman, not a shepherd, who has lost something, and it is a coin and not a sheep that has gotten lost. The woman turns her house upside down to find her lost coin, and when she does, she too throws a party with her equally incredulous neighbors.

So far, we have two similar stories. Something seemingly insignificant, but strangely precious, has been lost, and the one who has lost it will not rest until it is found. Now it is time for the third story, the story we mistakenly think is about the son.

Given the significance of triple repetition in Jewish culture, and given that the clear point of the first two stories is that Jesus' pursuit of and preference for spending time with "sinners" was that God desperately desires to find what has been lost, it is remarkable how easily we misread the point of the third story. This story is not about the son at all, or at least no more than the previous stories were primarily about a sheep and a coin. This story is about the father.

The story begins with a statement that confirms this: "There was a man who had two sons." The younger son has a plan. He is in line to receive a significant inheritance when his old man dies (evidently it's a pretty wealthy family). But who knows when that is going to be? He might be too old to really enjoy the wealth by then.

So he asks for it now. "Father, give me my share of the estate." In doing this, he is doing a lot more than just asking for money. Kenneth Bailey, a long-term missionary in rural Muslim communities, has written multiple books that are helpful in terms of understanding the cultural significance of this story.[1] He stresses that Jesus' audience would have been much like a rural Muslim community today. It would be a community based upon honor, protection of the honor of the community, the elders in the community, and the patriarchs (oldest men) in each family. Everything that happened in the community and within a family would be directed toward enhancing the honor of the patriarch, in this case, the father. To ask for the money now, years perhaps before the proper time, is a tremendously offensive thing for the son to do.

He is, in effect, saying to his father, "I wish you were dead. All you are to me is an obstacle to wealth." A son causing such offense in an honor-based rural community would face intense rejection. Not only would he not be given the money, he would be cast out by his family and the entire town. He had brought shame upon his father and the town, and he

---

1. Bailey, *The Cross and the Prodigal*.

would pay. The father would literally disown the son because of the son's behavior.

The movie *Fiddler on the Roof* contains a scene that shows what this would be like. Set in Russia at the turn of the twentieth century, the film features an orthodox Jewish family with a patriarch named Tevye. In this story, Tevye has no sons but several daughters, the older of which all marry men Tevye would not have chosen for them. A large part of the story is about, on the one hand, Tevye wrestling with his love for his daughters and his recognition that the world around him is changing, and on the other, his love and respect for the traditional faith and culture of his upbringing. With the first two daughters, Tevye comes to the understanding that things change, and he can love and accept his daughter's choices.

The third daughter, who is the apple of his eye, falls in love with a Gentile, a non-Jew, and desires to marry him. Tevye loves her deeply but cannot go this far. He disowns his beloved daughter. He will not allow her name to be spoken again by the family. He will not look upon her or acknowledge her presence.

This is what the father in Jesus' story should do. Instead, he gives his son the money he requests. And off the son goes. He foolishly burns through the money on wild living. When the money is gone, so are his options. He ends up working as a hired hand on a pig farm, a job that would be particularly offensive for this boy and the crowd listening to the story, since Jews would not eat pork or have any contact with pigs. In fact, he is so desperate that he begins to covet the food the pigs eat.

"Then he came to his senses," the story says. The son comes up with a plan. Pay close attention to his idea.

How many of my father's hired servants have food to spare while I am starving to death? I will set out and go to my father and say to him, "Father, I have sinned against heaven and against you. I am no longer worthy to be called your son; make me like on of your hired servants."[2]

Did you catch it? He is *not* planning on going home to try to gain back his place in the family as a son. That is gone. He knows that. That son is dead. "I am no longer worthy to be called your son." All he's hoping for, and what he's banking on, is that his father is a kinder master than the man he's working for now. He is not looking to get his father back, just to trade an uncaring master for a kinder one.

2. Luke 15:18–19.

Bailey talks about what the scene would be like as the son returns to the town. He describes the *Kezazah* ritual as a public shaming where the children and adults of the town would greet the disgraced one at the edge of town, barraging the person with rocks, stones, and verbal abuse. The son had not only shamed the father, he had brought shame upon the village, and now he would pay for it. He would get what he deserved. He would be met with physical and emotional pain. He would receive humiliation, shame, and rejection at the hands of the people of his village.

The listeners to this story would know exactly what was coming. They would have seen scenes like this play out in their own lives. This is how their world works.

If the son had the physical and emotional strength to endure this attack, he would come to the house. There he would be made to wait. The father would know that he was there, but still he would be made to wait outside. What is important here is protecting the honor of the father. *If* the father decided to allow the son into his presence (remember Tevye), the son would literally crawl into his presence, face to the ground, while the father would sit, unmoved, his honor intact. The crowd knew this part of the story, too.

But that is not how this story ends.

"But while he [the son] was still a long way off, his father saw him and was filled with compassion for him; he ran to his son, threw his arms around him, and kissed him."[3]

Jesus' listeners would have no idea what to do with that sentence. Nothing in their social experience could make sense of what the father has just done. It was socially incomprehensible on so many levels.

Adult men *never* ran. That was for children, for babies. It was undignified.

This father ran.

Adult men, particularly patriarchs, did not show emotion in public, physically or otherwise. They did not talk to women and children outside of the home.

This father throws his arms around his son, embraces him, and kisses him.

Why run out to meet him while he's still a long way off? Surely, one reason is the father's unwillingness to wait. He clearly has not performed

3. Luke 15:20.

the expected disowning of his son. His son, though dead to the community, has remained alive to the father's heart, and he cannot wait to show that. But there's a more practical reason. The father knows that *Kezazah* awaits his son. In reaching his son on the outskirts of the village, the father reaches him before the barrage of derision, shame, and hate is poured out upon him. He has run out to protect his son as well as to demonstrate his love for him.

The father's extraordinary actions are not finished.

The son launches into his prepared speech. "Father I have sinned against heaven and against you. I am no longer fit to be called your son." He never gets to the end.

The father cuts him off and calls to his servants, "Bring the best robe. Bring my ring. Bring him shoes. Kill the best calf, the one we've been saving for a special occasion. My son was dead and is alive! My son was lost and is found!" The robe and ring are significant. The father is not just saying, "My son is covered in pig manure; get him some decent clothes." The robe and ring are signs of the honor and dignity that the father, as the righteous patriarch of the family, has in the community. He is removing them and placing them upon his filthy, shamed, dishonored son.

The father is rejecting the honor-and-shame calculus of the community. According to that system, for honor to be preserved, shame must be heaped upon the son. He is also rejecting the calculus of the son. "All my dishonor can hope for is a place among the servants." The father intercedes on behalf of the son in front of the community. He deflects the shame and punishment due the son by publicly humiliating himself. He rejects the calculated works-righteousness of the son and offers grace.

"Come home! You are my son! Let us celebrate! All is well!"

Three stories. Three times the hero of the story is not the one who gets lost and figures out how to get back home. The hero each time is the one who goes to great lengths to find what has been lost, to restore things to how they should be. In the case of the father, this comes with great cost. It requires setting aside the honor, vengeance, and retribution that justice offers and instead taking up the shame and humiliation that would make reconciliation possible.

A short time later, Jesus would do the same thing on the cross. Sin carries a great cost for the sinner. We experience guilt and shame and, most important, we are cut off from relationship with God. Preserving justice and honor would not have cost Hosea, the father, or God much of anything. All that would be required is letting Gomer, the son, and us get what was deserved. Reconciliation costs everything for Hosea, for the father, and for God.

"You will call me 'my husband.' You will no longer call me 'my master.'"

"My son was dead and now is alive."

"God demonstrates his love for us in this: While we were still sinners, Christ died for us."

Come Home

A STORY IS TOLD of a wealthy father who had a falling out with his son. In anger and humiliation, the son had left home, swearing never to return. Months and then years passed. The father ached to be reconciled with his son but had no idea where he was or how to contact him. Since this was the era before blogs, Internet data searches, or Facebook, the father had limited options.

He hit upon a plan. Money was no object, so he contacted the advertising department of the main newspaper in every major city in the country. He would take out the same ad in each one. The ad simply said this:

Paul, come home. Son, all is forgiven.

Included was a toll free phone number, in case his son was out of money. The ad appeared across the country the following Sunday. Monday morning, the phone service set up to field the call to the toll free number was overwhelmed with calls, all from young men named, Paul, all hoping that the message was intended for them.

Embrace

THE PIVOTAL MOMENT IN the story of the prodigal son and his father is the moment of embrace. "But while he [the son] was still far off, his father saw him and was filled with compassion; he ran and put his arms around him and kissed him."[1] In 1996, Croatian theologian Miroslav Volf published the profound work, *Exclusion and Embrace.*[2] The book covers a range of issues dealing with Otherness (How do I interact with those who are different than me?), what it means to be human, and the obstacles and possibilities for genuine reconciliation. It is at times a dense book, and it is often achingly beautiful. Volf says that the biblical story that inspired the work and served as its foundation is the story of the prodigal son. Further, he chooses *embrace* as the representative event, or symbol, for "the whole realm of human relations in which the interplay between the self and the other takes place."[3]

He did not write this book in some vacuum of academic detachment. Much of the book was physically written during, and all of it must be seen through the lens of, the war in the Balkans that engulfed his Croatian people in the 1990s. "Can I embrace a Serb?" is a question he asks in the first paragraph of the book. Embrace is a philosophical concept to Volf. It is also a theological truth, as well as a gut-wrenching debate in his day-to-day life.

In discussing embrace as a physical act, he breaks the movement down into its component parts. I'm not going to mention them all here or give them the depth of consideration that he does. I would like to note a few of his points, however.

Opening. The first movement of embrace is the opening of my arms toward you, or the father's arms toward the son. In the opening of my arms, I am saying a few things. I am *reaching out toward, making room for within,* and *inviting.*

Arms reaching out initiate the embrace. I am making a move toward you. The move is unambiguous. As a white, middle-aged male, I am all too

1. Luke 15:20.
2. Volf, *Exclusion and Embrace.*
3. Ibid., 140.

familiar with the awkward moment of greeting where I debate, "Should I extend my hand for a handshake, or my arms for an embrace? What is this person going to do? What's appropriate here?" The outreached arms are not asking those questions. They are decisive. I have moved toward you. I have committed to the possibility of embrace.

When I open my arms to you, I am also making room within myself to include you. I am not walling myself off. Again drawing from my up-tight white maleness, I am no stranger to the sort-of-embraces folks like me often give. For example, the side hug, with both parties standing next to one another, touching sides, and lightly putting arms around one another. There's also the lean in, with both parties standing at some distance from one another and bending stiffly at the hips so that the shoulders barely touch. This is not the kind of embrace Volf is talking about. That is not the embrace of the father and the son.

The embrace that Volf describes is one that opens fully. It is an extending of the arms that is an invitation: "Come in." There is no need to ask permission; the door is open. In fact, Volf describes the open arms as a "soft knock" on the door of the other.

Waiting. This is a key and easily overlooked idea. The embrace of love, the embrace of reconciliation and healing, waits. Once the arms have been extended, the invitation given, the door of the other gently knocked upon, I wait. If I were to push ahead, the embrace would become coercion, maybe even violence. In sexual politics, the difference between consensual sex and rape is the refusal to allow the other to say "yes" or the failure to accept "no." In contrast, when I embrace you truly, I wait to see if you are open to the embrace. I pause. You are a partner in the embrace. It is not forced upon you.

Holding. Returning again to my oh-so-awkward pseudo-embraces, the true embrace will have nothing to do with them. Not only will it not be satisfied with the side hug or the lean in, but it also is not the embrace of a millisecond. It lingers. I will confess that I have extended more of these kinds of embraces than I've allowed myself to receive. The holding nature of the true embrace is what happens when one of my daughters has hurt herself playing outside or is distraught at a failed art project. When I embrace in this way, I allow Bailey or Rachel to *melt into my arms.* Think about that phrase, "melt into my arms." In lingering in the embrace, I allow my daughters to, in a real way, *lose themselves* in the embrace.

I suspect that this is both the most powerful element of true embrace, what the son experienced in the arms of the father, and the reason that it is easier for me to extend it to you than to receive it from you. When we think about embrace as an idea that tells us something about God's movement toward and for us on the cross, this is the moment of conversion, or repentance. This is the moment where, to truly experience the healing of the embrace, I have to give myself over to it, to you, to God.

This is tremendously hard for virtually all of us. I want to maintain all of myself. I want to be autonomous. I want to be able to figure it out, to pull myself up by my bootstraps, to get the job done on my own. Allowing myself to be held is precisely how I acknowledge that none of that can work. It is an acknowledgement of need. It is my allowing you or God to be something for me that I cannot be for myself.

Of course, that is also why it is both so hard and so good to be held. Humanity has resisted the embrace of God for all of its history. That is one way of thinking about the Fall. Collectively, and individually, we are the children standing rigidly, stubbornly refusing to melt into the loving arms of the parent's embrace. When we do so, we walk away unchanged and unhealed. Not for lack of invitation, for lack of arms held open, for room made by God, but because of us.

When we receive the Grace of God extended by Jesus through the cross, we allow ourselves to be held. We open up *ourselves* to God, in response to God's opening to us.

> "*This mutual embrace—God embracing our pain and ugliness,*
> *and humanity embracing God's mercy and beauty*
> *—creates the possibility of a new beginning . . .*"[4]
> —Brian D. McLaren

---

4. McLaren, *Everything Must Change.*

This Father Had *Another* Son

PERHAPS NO STORY OF Jesus' has captured the imagination of Christians over the centuries like the story of the lost or prodigal son. As has already been made clear, I think that story is one of the pivotal metaphors or narratives for understanding Jesus. What gets easily lost in the beauty and emotion of this story of a father's reconciliation with his younger, wayward son is the fact that there is another member of the family, the older son.

The older son's story is often ignored for at least a few reasons. For one thing, it's not the center of the action. It almost reads as an afterthought to the longer story of the younger son. Perhaps more important, however, is the fact that this son's story does not emotionally satisfy like his brother's. This son is not a sympathetic character, and his story does not seem to end well. The very best that could be said for it is that it ends without resolution, but it seems very likely that it ends badly.

Finally, and in our present culture's desire to be inclusive and all-affirming (and I count myself here), there is the fact that, if the other son's story speaks to the possibility of forgiveness and reconciliation for all, the older son's story speaks to the possibility of rejection and exclusion. As the story unfolds, I think we'll see that these possibilities are responses that the son seems to make and not the father, but for some of us, even the possibility that any could be "outside the party" is difficult to process.

Here is how this part of the story goes.

Following the father's powerful acts of shame-bearing and reconciliation toward his younger son, the father calls for a celebration. "Kill the fatted calf," he orders, "my son was lost and has been found."[1] It is time to celebrate! Family members, friends, and neighbors all gather to both rejoice with the father and themselves be reconciled to his wayward son. While the essential rupture of relationship had been with the father, in an ancient, shame-honor based village like Jesus describes here, the son's actions would have alienated him from the entire village. Everyone would have shared in the rejection and shunning, and now, everyone was invited to the celebration of return.

---

1. Luke 15:23–24.

One key individual is prominently absent. The father had *two* sons. One son had not demanded his inheritance. One son had not left home. One son had dutifully worked for his father all this time. The older son.

That son is furious.

He comes in from the fields after another hard day's labor, another day "earning" what would someday be his. Instead of the normal end-of-day routine, he hears the sounds of a celebration. He asks one of his dad's servants, "What's going on?"

"Your brother has come, and your father has killed the fatted calf because he has him back safe and sound,"[2] the servant replies.

Not only is the older son angry, but he also refuses to go into the house. So what does the Father do, this father who ran to his disgraced son, who bore the disdain of the village for and with that son?

Why, he again goes to his son, of course! The father "went out and pleaded with him"[3] to come in. The son is unmoved, both by the father's movement toward him and by his brother's return. It isn't fair. He's worked all these years, meticulously following his father's instructions, and never once had a party to celebrate. And now his wayward brother, who ought to be dead to the entire family (you certainly get the sense he is to the older brother), returns and everyone is giddy with joy.

The father is heartbroken at this, I believe, for two reasons. He says, "My son, you are always with me, and everything I have is yours, but we had to celebrate and be glad, because this brother of yours was dead and is alive again; he was lost and is found."[4] He is saddened by the hardness of heart from one son to the other, and he is hurt by the inability of his older son to want good to come to his brother.

I think he is also saddened by the fact that the older brother has missed the point all these years. "You are always with me, and everything I have is yours," the father says. All his life, the son has worked, followed the rules, and "slaved" for his father, never realizing that "all that I [the father] have" was his, merely because he was his son.

In essence, *both* sons have missed the love of the father, both sons have missed the value of relationship and seen the father as a means to the things they desire. "You've never thrown me a party," the older son

2. Luke 15:27.

3. Luke 15:28.

4. Luke 15:31–32.

says. The sons are not that different, they just chose different strategies to get what they both wanted: the father's wealth and property without the father himself. One did it by brazenly asking and then leaving home, the other by slavishly working. In both cases, the one thing the truly needed, the one thing of true value, the love of the father, was lost to them. It was lost not because it wasn't offered, but because neither one wanted it.

There are two sobering messages here. It is possible to miss out on the party, on the Kingdom of God, on heaven. As the story ends, the older son is still outside, arms crossed and defiant. It seems, as persistent as the father's love is (remember, he leaves the party to plead with this son), it is possible to say "no." It is possible to have a heart so hardened to love and grace that it is unmovable. That certainly seems to be the case for this son.

Additionally, the son who ultimately remains on the outside, who in all likelihood represents a choice for hell over heaven, was the *upstanding* son. A stunning truth about Jesus' interactions in the Gospels, and one that should give those of us who have grown up in the Church pause, is that he *never* speaks words of anger or judgment at those whom we normally associate as being outsiders to faith: sinners, prostitutes, non-Jews. *All* of his warnings about pending judgment are toward highly observant, religious folks. I am guessing, if you put the older son in our context, that in addition to his hard work in the fields, he never missed church on Sunday or drank or cursed or participated in anything that would compromise his being a *good Christian.*

Could it be that I could go to church all my life and be left standing, arms crossed in anger outside the door? Personally, I spent a lot of my early years in exactly that spot.

Another of Jesus' parables, and my response to it, illustrates this.

Jesus tells a story about a man who hires workers to work in his field: day laborers. He hires some at eight o'clock in the morning and promises them a good day's wage. At noon, he sees some more men standing around and hires them, too. Throughout the day, anyone he sees, even those he sees with only an hour or so to go in the day, get hired.

At the end of the day, all the workers line up to get their pay. To everyone's surprise, the men who'd worked only an hour get a full day's pay, as do the men who worked half a day, as do the ones who get exactly what they were promised: a day's pay for a day's work.

I vividly remember hating this story as a kid. This just wasn't fair. Why would the owner of the field (God), be so generous with people who *didn't deserve* it? They should get something, but not as much as those who'd *earned* what they got. Looking back, the internal source of my frustration is easy to see. I was pretty sure my place in the parable was one of the full-day laborers. I'd always gone to church. I didn't get in trouble. I knew God loved me and I pretty much thought he should, because I'd earned it. I was the older son.

Years later, after several personal failures had caused me to see myself with new eyes, I returned to this parable. Now it struck me as beautiful. I was not the eight o'clock hire after all; I was the five o'clock in the afternoon hire on whom God showered mercy undeserved. I have come to believe we all are. When we get right down to it, none of us get what we deserve from God. We get much more.

The trick is, can we, like the younger son, recognize that and melt into the father's arms, or will we stand outside the door demanding *fair* treatment, when really something much better is offered? Can we realize that, in the end, all of us are latecomers to the field, standing in line, waiting to receive love and mercy that far exceeds anything we could possibly deserve?

Hope for the Hollow Man

MANY CONSIDER T. S. Eliot to be the most important English-language poet of the twentieth century. He won a Nobel Prize for his poetry, and his poem *The Wasteland* [1] is often referred to as *the* defining poem of Western Civilization in a century that brought two world wars and a nuclear arms race that threatened all human life. In Eliot's early poetry, *The Wasteland* and *The Hollow Men* [2] for example, there is despair at the emptiness of human existence. Eliot wrote these poems in England after World War I, a war that traumatized all of the world, but Europe in particular, with its horrendous loss of life. He also was in a disintegrating marriage and on the brink of a nervous breakdown.

A number of things led to a changed perspective on Eliot's part, but chief among them was his conversion to Christianity. In Christianity, he found a hope for the future and the presence of Love in the present. He described it as a returning home and somehow recognizing it as home, even though he'd never been there before. The early T. S. Eliot poetry bears a striking resemblance to the "nought" that Walker Percy described. The latter poetry, also like Percy's works, reflects a hope found outside of ourselves, in the Love of God for us.

In a similar way, the late-twentieth century British writer Malcolm Muggeridge considered himself to be an atheist cynic. He thought faith was a sham. While making a documentary for the BBC, he met Mother Theresa in Calcutta. Watching her serve the poorest of the poor in her Home for the Dying shook Muggeridge to the core. Late in life, at the age of sixty-six, Muggeridge converted to Christianity. Like Eliot, he'd found a way out of the cynicism and despair of a world darkened by two world wars, the Holocaust, the atom bomb, and the Cold War, and that way out was named Jesus.

1. Eliot, *Complete Poems and Plays: 1909–1950.*
2. Ibid.

Buechner Tells the Story of the Prodigal

ONE OF MY FAVORITE authors, Frederick Buechner, describes in the first person the emotional state of the son in the story of the Prodigal Son in his essay, "The Truth of Stories."[1] In words far better than I could ever find, he describes the scene. I quote him here at length:

> Once upon a time, for instance, I got fed up and left home, got the hell out, no matter why. I bought a one-way ticket for as far as there was to go and got off at the last stop. I spent myself down to where I didn't have the price of a cup of coffee, and that was not the worst of it. The worst of it was that I didn't give a damn because there wasn't anything else I wanted even if I'd had the price. There wasn't anything to see I hadn't seen. There wasn't anything to do I hadn't done. There wasn't anything to lose I hadn't lost. The only worse thing than being fed up with the world is being fed up with yourself. I envied the pigs their slops because at least they knew what they were hungry for whereas I was starving to death and had no idea why. All I know was that the emptiness inside me was bigger than I was. So I went back. As I might have guessed the old man was waiting for me. I was ready to crawl to him, say anything he wanted. He looked smaller than I remembered him. He looked small and breakable against the tall sky. His coat didn't look warm enough. It lapped around his shins. We ran the last length between us if you could call the way he did it running. I couldn't get a word out. My mouth was pushed crooked against his chest, he held me so tight. I was blinded by whatever blinded me. I could still hear though. I could hear the thump of his old ticker through the skimpy coat. I could hear his voice break.[2]

For me, several lines jump out:
"There wasn't anything to lose that I hadn't lost."
"All I know was that the emptiness inside me was bigger than I was."
"He held me so tight."
"I could hear his voice break."

---

1. Buechner, *The Clown in the Belfry*, 133–34.
2. Ibid.

Thielicke in Hamburg, Post-World War II

GERMANY IN THE 1950s had been hit with wave after wave. They had suffered devastating defeat in World War I, in terms of both lives and humiliation. Less than thirty years later, they experienced an even more horrific war, in which Germany first endured the Nazi regime and then the crushing defeat of the Nazis by the Allied Forces. Immediately on World War II's heels, Europe, and nowhere more than Germany, was plunged into the Cold War, the standoff between the democratic West and the Soviet Union and its satellite states, known as the Communist Block. Germany was literally split in two—East Germany and West Germany—with Berlin, deep in East Germany, being itself split, with West Berlin dependent upon airlifted supplies. In West Germany, postwar starvation was soon replaced, as it was around Western Europe and in America, with rampant materialism.

Germany, also like all of Western Europe, was rapidly becoming post-Christian. Germany was once a nation that produced so much of Christianity's thinking about God that to pursue a graduate degree in theology in the United States one was required to learn German. Martin Luther, the father of the Protestant Reformation, was a German. By the 1950s, massive churches across Germany, once full and vibrant, sat almost empty. Sparse dozens worshiped in churches that once held thousands.

In Hamburg, Germany, in the mid-1950s, a theology professor preached a series of sermons based upon the parables of Jesus. Services that started in a small church had to be moved to the largest cathedral in town, holding four thousand people. When the cathedral on Sunday could not accommodate the crowds, midweek meetings were scheduled where the professor would repeat Sunday's sermon word for word. The professor was Helmut Thielicke, and the sermons that drew thousands of people, young and old, churched and unchurched, were centered around his sermon on the prodigal son, or as he referred to it, the parable of the waiting father. What was a distinguished theology professor doing preaching sermons based upon "stories"? He believed that the secret to understanding God, in spite of his position as a professor of theology, was not to be found in theology or in textbooks. He pointed his listeners and readers toward the parables of Jesus. The parables were pictures of God, and no picture was more central to Thielicke than the parable of the prodigal son.

These sermons, entitled *God's Picturebook* and *The Waiting Father,*[1] in its English translation, are often considered some of the best preaching of the twentieth century. In his sermon on the prodigal son, Thielicke drew clear comparisons between the son's situation in the "far off country" to the situation of the postwar, post-poverty, post-Christian West of the 1950s. He talked to a Germany that he said was seeking to fill its "emptied and peace-less selves" with things (freezers and TVs—this was the 1950s), philosophy, and the arts, but was really just a "blown-up nothingness."[2] He compared this to the starving son in a far off land, having blown through his share of the family inheritance and now staring longingly at pig slop.

He concludes his sermon with a series of beautiful and powerful statements, made all the more so by the place and time in which he said them. "The ultimate theme of this story, therefore, is not the prodigal son, but the Father who finds us. The ultimate theme is not the faithlessness of men, but the faithfulness of God."[3] Speaking of the moment when the son "comes to his senses" standing in a pigsty and decides to head home, he stresses, "The repentance of the lost son is therefore not something merely negative (focused upon his sin, failure, and shame). In the last analysis it is not merely disgust; it is above all homelessness; not just turning away from something, but turning back home . . . The ultimate secret of this story is this: there is a homecoming for us all because there is a home."[4]

1. Thielicke, *The Waiting Father,* 27.
2. Ibid., 27.
3. Ibid., 28.
4. Ibid., 29.

Jesus and Peter, Before and After the Cross
and Resurrection

JESUS' DISCIPLE PETER IS a figure who hovers on the edge of the story before and after the death of Jesus. In many ways, Peter has been Jesus' go-to guy. He is a leader among Jesus' twelve closest followers, often being the one to speak up and voice an opinion for the rest. He is the first to declare that Jesus is Lord, Son of God. At the same time, he regularly puts his foot in his mouth, at times even being rebuked by Jesus for interfering with Jesus' intended mission.

The night of Jesus' arrest, Jesus shares a meal with his twelve closest friends. At the meal, Jesus says that, in the coming hours, all of them will desert him. Peter protests that he would never do that. Jesus replies that Peter is wrong, and on that very night Peter will specifically deny knowing Jesus three separate times. Peter is indignant. He is too brave and too devoted for this to even be thinkable.

Of course, Jesus was right. After the agonizing prayer in the Garden of Gethsemane, during which Peter, James, and John fall asleep after being asked to accompany Jesus, Jesus is arrested. Peter rashly resists the arrest, slashing the ear of a Roman soldier clean off, but Jesus tells him to put away his sword. Jesus is brought, in the middle of the night, before the Jewish Sanhedrin (a religious supreme court, of sorts). Peter lurks in the outer courtyard along with a fair number of others. Being from the Galilean countryside, just as Jesus was, the others with whom he's milling around recognize his accent and begin to say, "Hey, you've got the same accent as that Jesus guy. You must be one of his friends. What is the deal?" (Their Galilean accents would stand out in Jerusalem like a native of the Bronx sitting at a Seattle Starbucks or a Georgian having breakfast in a Chicago diner.) Fearing for himself, Peter each time responds, "I don't know what you're talking about. I have no idea who he is."

Scripture says that, after Peter's third denial, he leaves and goes off by himself, weeping bitterly. We've already mentioned, in discussing the parables of the lost sheep, the lost coin, and the prodigal son, the significance in Jewish culture of saying something three times. In three times denying any relationship with Jesus, Peter has spoken with binding emphasis. When push came to shove, Jesus was right. Peter has broken and denied the most precious relationship in the world to him. He is beside himself with remorse, guilt, and shame.

Jesus dies alone on the cross, abandoned by his friends, with the exception of a handful of women who courageously remain by his side. Three days later, he rises from the dead. Again, these beautiful women are the first to learn the wonderful truth, having been the last to stay with Jesus at his death. In each Gospel account, the women are instructed to pass on the good news to the now eleven disciples (Judas, who betrayed Jesus to the Jewish authorities, having hung himself). In Mark, the women are told to "Go tell his disciples *and Peter* that Jesus is going on ahead of them to Galilee and will meet them there." Why *and Peter*? Why is he singled out?

The Gospel of John, I believe, tells us why. Here the scene picks up with Peter and the disciples out fishing at dawn on the Sea of Galilee. This is the place where Peter had first met Jesus. This is where, after speaking to a large crowd, Jesus had taken a skeptical Peter fishing. This was on a hot morning after a night when Peter had caught nothing. Jesus had revealed himself to be a fishing novice by saying, "Maybe you didn't catch any fish last night because you were throwing your nets off the wrong side of the boat. Try the other side." Peter humored foolish Jesus but knew that had nothing to do with it. Except that suddenly his nets had almost burst and his boat almost sank with the largest catch of fish he'd ever seen! Thus started Peter's enthrallment with the man who would turn his life upside down.

Now he was back in the same region, fishing again.

Again, it had been a long and fruitless night. They'd not caught anything. (One begins to wonder that, for a man whose profession is Professional Fisherman, Peter pretty regularly seems to be a failure at catching fish.) In the predawn light, Peter and the others see a man standing on the shore looking out toward them. The man calls out, "Have you caught any fish?" Sheepishly, they reply that they have not.

"Why don't you try throwing your net over the other side of the boat? Maybe you'll have better luck." They try and they do. For the second time, Peter is faced with more fish than his nets and boat can handle.

That phrase, "Why don't you try throwing your net over the other side?" It wouldn't have meant anything to the others, but Peter knew exactly what it meant. He knew exactly who he had heard say this before. It was Jesus. It was the man he loved. It was the man he believed to be the Son of God. The man he'd denied bitterly and decisively. Jesus was waiting for them, for him, on the shore.

Peter is beside himself. In one of the funnier scenes in the Gospels, he puts all of his clothes back on (it's hot, hard work, fishing in the Middle East) and *then* dives into the water to swim to shore. The rest just take the boat on in because they are only one hundred yards from the shore. You can almost picture Peter thrashing and floundering in all of his clothes as the boat sails in next to him.

On the shore, they share a meal. Jesus cooks some of the fish for them. This is a very relational thing to do. Then he asks Peter three questions, and three times Peter answers. Three. Curious.

"Do you love me?"

"Yes, you know I love you, Jesus."

How odd, to ask the same thing three times. It is odd unless you are Jewish, of course. It is odd unless you know that stating three times binds the speaker to his words, unless you know that, a few days earlier, the speaker had three times denied his love for Jesus. In asking Peter three times, "Do you love me?" Jesus is lovingly allowing Peter to unbind himself from his denial. Jesus is healing their relationship.

Try convincing Peter that the heart of the cross and the resurrection wasn't relational reconciliation. He had experienced it firsthand.

In the hours before Jesus' death, two of Jesus' closest followers publicly betrayed Jesus or denied any relationship with him: Judas and Peter. Peter weeps with grief. So does Judas. Judas hangs himself. Peter does not. Judas becomes one of the most reviled figures in human history. Peter goes on to be one of the pivotal individuals in the spreading of the Good News of Jesus to the world. Why did they end up so differently when their sin in those hours was so similar?

The Bible doesn't say, but I am left with one question, given what we see throughout all of the Bible about God and what we see in the Gospels about Jesus: "Is not the only real difference between the two that Peter kept alive just enough hope to stick around until Jesus rose from the dead and offered him forgiveness?" Had Judas not hung himself, what would Jesus have said to him after the resurrection?

Hilasterion

S OME OF THE QUESTIONS that arise for folks thinking about Jesus' death come from words like Paul's in Romans 3:25, where Jesus is said to be, in many translations, the *atoning sacrifice* for our sins. Is he a sacrifice to God? But isn't he God himself? Is God sacrificing himself to himself? What in God demands this sacrifice?

Less often asked is the question, "Is *atoning sacrifice* the only or best term here?" In the original Greek, the term that is often translated as *atoning sacrifice* is *hilasterion*. There is no question that *atoning sacrifice* is one of the acceptable translations of this word. But the word itself means *mercy seat*. The mercy seat was the cover of the Ark of the Covenant, kept in the Holy of Holies within the Temple. It was the place where the High Priest would sprinkle the blood of the sacrificed animal on the Day of Atonement. The mercy seat was the place where reconciliation between God and Israel happened.

Here is the question: Does the word *hilasterion* mean the sacrifice that happens at the mercy seat, or does it mean the place itself? Do you see the difference? If the first meaning is correct, Jesus is the animal that is slaughtered. If the second is correct, Jesus is the place where reconciliation happens. Jesus is the place where God and humanity are reconciled.

Both definitions have merit. Using the first certainly points one toward an understanding of Jesus' death built around God requiring blood in order to forgive and Jesus providing that blood. Using the second points one more toward an understanding of Jesus' death that stresses Jesus as the vehicle through which God-Humanity reconciliation is made possible, but it doesn't necessarily mean that was brought about by Jesus becoming a slaughtered sacrifice.

For those offended by the idea of God demanding blood to be satisfied and welcoming Jesus' blood as acceptable, this second definition, which has substantial biblical support, offers a way to understand verses like Romans 3:25 in a new light. Also, for those troubled by how God can be both the one who demands sacrifice and the one who is sacrificed, this alternate definition may be of help.

The mercy seat is where reconciliation occurred. The cross is the place where reconciliation occurs. It is the place where the father humiliates himself and takes upon himself the prodigal son's shame to bring about reconciliation. It is the place where Hosea pays the price for his wife's freedom and extends to her the open arms of reconciliation. A price is still being paid, the cross is still essential, but the emphasis has shifted.

More often than not, a Bible you pick up is going to translate *hilasterion* as atoning sacrifice. Many Bibles, if they provide footnotes, will also say, "or place of atonement" in the footnote. I'm not arguing for "place of atonement" to the exclusion of "atoning sacrifice," but, most of the time, we have only thought of things in terms of Jesus as the sacrifice itself. I *am* arguing that both definitions need to be part of the dialogue of the meaning of the cross.

A Game with Words

Rules: Sum up the Bible in as few words as possible.

FIRST TRY

"I *am*."
"Naked and not ashamed."
"I was afraid because I was naked, so I hid."
"On that day, God made a covenant with Abraham."
"I have heard you crying out in your misery and have set about to rescue you."
"The people walking in darkness have seen a great light."
"God became flesh and made his dwelling among us."
"I lay down my life."
"He is risen."
"Behold, I make all things new."

SECOND TRY

Embrace.
Rejection.
Reconciling embrace.

THIRD TRY

hesed

Already, but Not Yet

S O, WE ARE DONE, right? Jesus reconciles us to God, we can go to heaven, and that's that.

No. Remember, shalom is a great, broad, all-inclusive idea of wholeness. The apostle Paul, writing in 2 Corinthians, says, "All this is from God, who was reconciling the world to himself in Christ and gave us the ministry of reconciliation."[1] Elsewhere, he says that, because of Christ "the new creation has come."[2] Not that I'm a new creation or you're a new creation, but that creation is made new and is in the process of being made new.

A phrase that gets used in describing this idea is that the Kingdom of God is "already, but not yet." It is already here, but not yet fully come or fully complete. From the moment of conception, new life is in the mother's womb, but it has not fully come until the moment of birth.

One of the most common metaphors through which Christians talk about the cross of Christ is that we stand guilty before God, the judge, and that Jesus, the innocent one, has intervened with God, taking our punishment and allowing us to go free. There are certainly things about this metaphor that are useful, but one of the unspoken conclusions of the image is not. Think about a court proceeding. If the defendant goes free, he leaves the courtroom. The judge has freed him. He may be grateful. He may sing the judge's praises, but he leaves and likely never sees her again. He "gets on with his life," and the judge gets on with hers. (Now, I fully admit that fans of this metaphor would never make this point overtly. I'm just saying that this is where the logic of the metaphor naturally takes you.)

If, instead, we think of the cross in terms of metaphors like Hosea and Gomer or the father and his wayward son, the cross doesn't end things. It is not so much the closing of a chapter, but the beginning of the real story. "Let's get on about the business of being husband and wife together," or, "Son, it's so good to have you home again. Let me show you what we've done with the place while you've been gone." The cross, in these metaphors, opens the door to a relationship. (Again, fans of the courtroom metaphor

1. 2 Corinthians 5:19.
2. 2 Corinthians 5:17.

believe the same thing; they just have to switch metaphors midstream to make that happen).

What does it look like to walk with God in this "new creation"? What is it like to be given "the ministry of reconciliation"?

Pools or Rivers

Picture this. Imagine yourself flying into Dallas, Texas, and looking out of the window as you descend. As you look down, you see mile after mile of neighborhoods with beautiful homes and fenced-in backyards, many of which have what? They have a swimming pool.

While this is not a perfect metaphor, I believe that, in many ways, many of us picture becoming a Christian like purchasing our very own "Jesus swimming pool." It's ours. That pool is going to really feel great after a tough day at work or school. It is a great way to find some tranquility. We can get in and out when we want. We can invite the neighbors over for a swim or we can just swim in it by ourselves. Maybe the neighbors will invite us over for a swim in their pool. They just got a new slide. We can regulate the temperature and have just the right number of pool toys. That first summer, we'll probably swim in it every day, but as the years go along, it will sit empty most of the time, unless it's a really hot day and we need to cool off or maybe the kids come to visit and want to take a dip.

In a lot of ways, that is pretty similar to how we think Christian faith works. What I'm saying here is a caricature, but I think there is a fair bit of truth in it. Why did Jesus come to earth? He came to die for me, so I could have a personal relationship with him. What does he want from me? That I pray (privately) to God. That I spend time reading the Bible. That I keep my life clean. No swearing, drinking, sleeping around, certainly no voting for *that* party. Once a week I should go to church with other people who have personal relationships with Jesus, and we will listen to a talk about how to improve our personal relationships with Jesus. Afterwards, we'll ask ourselves how we're doing and we'll all smile, no matter how we are doing, and say, "Really great. How about you?"

What about my neighbors? Well, I'm more than happy to tell them how pleased I am with my personal relationship with Jesus and ask them to think about getting one, too. I don't want to be pushy though; it's really their personal choice after all.

Faith is private, like my fenced-in pool. I share about it from time to time, just like I invite folks over for a swim after work, but let's not get carried away. What Christianity is primarily about, in this metaphor, is improving me, my behavior, and my experience of life. Having Jesus in my life has really helped me. I'm much more disciplined now. I'm getting along better with my wife. It's been a definite plus, just like the property value of my house went up when I put in the pool. They've both definitely added a sense of class and respectability to my life. It's hard to remember how I ever got along without them.

Now I'd like you to picture flying in to where I live, Portland, Oregon. As you descend and look out the left side of the plane, as I mentioned earlier, you may be initially terrified by Mount Hood, which appears to be about ten feet away from the wing of the plane. Off to the right side of the plane, as you descend, your view is dominated again by water, only this water is very different. It's the Columbia River. The Columbia starts in the mountains of Canada and pours down through Idaho, Washington, and Oregon and on to the Pacific Ocean. It is massive, powerful, and definitely going somewhere.

If you were to grab a raft and jump in the Columbia, you'd be in for quite a ride. It would take you by constantly changing landscapes. Sometimes cascading rapids, other times slow moving, but always something new. You would float past mountain logging camps, wheat fields, small communities, and major cities. You would be on the move. Heading toward the ocean.

This is what I believe becoming a Christian really is. Not building a safe, private Jesus pool in the backyard, but walking over to the river's edge, taking Jesus' hand, and jumping in. There's no telling where the current will take you, who you will meet out there, or if it will always be calm and easy. But you can be sure it is going somewhere. It is joining in the vast story of "God reconciling the world" that started with the Fall and will continue to the end of time. God is inviting you to become a part of God's vast story.

It is not safe. It is not sterile. It is not something you can control, getting in and out whenever the mood strikes you. It can't be contained in your heart, your color-coded journal, and certainly not your backyard.

It is a story that was moving through human history before you were born and will continue on after you are gone, but it is also a story in which you are invited to take part. It has a direction, as surely as a river rolls to the sea. It is about God's re-creation of all that is. It is about God's restoration of *shalom.* Your personal salvation and, very likely, the cleaning up of the mess in your life are *big* parts of that. But just like a small mountain stream joins another and then another and then the river as they cascade down, God's story with you just begins with the start of your personal relationship with Jesus. That's the first couple of pages of the first chapter, not the book itself.

What follows are some examples of what that might look like in the world.

Parties for Prostitutes

CHRISTIAN SOCIOLOGIST, AUTHOR, AND social activist Tony Campolo tells a story that I first heard years ago. He wrote about it in his book *The Kingdom of God Is a Party*.[1] Campolo was in Hawaii speaking at a conference. Tony is from Philadelphia, so his body was very confused about the time. He would go to bed on Hawaiian time each night but wake up on Philadelphia time, which was two or three in the morning. A diner across the street from the hotel was open all night, and so it became his nightly haunt: A place to get a snack, read a little, and while away the time until everyone else woke up.

The first night, Tony discovered that he was not the only person in town awake. Late in the night, several provocatively clad women arrived at the diner, filling up the booths near Tony's. The local prostitutes were finished with work for the night and were getting together. As the week progressed, the same routine repeated itself each night. Tony would wake up way too early, make his way to the diner to read, and after a time, would be surrounded by a group of prostitutes.

Tony tried not to eavesdrop, but the women were pretty loud and paid no attention to him, so it was hard not to take in a fair bit of their conversations. They would talk about the johns they'd been with. Some were jerks, others just lonely and pathetic. They would talk about their pimps. Some would talk about their homes, about trying to keep families afloat any way they could. Others were on their own, alone. All of the stories were sad, and all of them were hard.

One woman in particular struck Tony. She mournfully talked about the fact that the next day would be her birthday and that she'd spend it like the previous year's and the years' before that: alone, uncelebrated by anyone. It would be just another day selling herself to get by, just like every day.

When they all left, Tony couldn't stop thinking about that woman and her birthday. And then he had an idea. He asked the owner of the diner if he knew what her name was. He did. He asked him if he'd be up for helping him with a project. He was. Together, they began to plot a

---

1. Campolo, *The Kingdom of God Is a Party*, 3–9.

birthday party. Tony bought balloons, streamers, and presents. The owner baked a cake with the woman's name on it. He cleaned the place up a bit.

The next night, Tony was back at his booth. Right on schedule, the prostitutes rolled in. Only this time, they walked into a diner that had been transformed. It was festive. It was beautiful. There were squeals of delight. Laughter. Stories. Tears.

Toward the end, the owner of the diner asked Tony who he was and why he had done this. Tony sheepishly replied that he was a pastor. The owner couldn't believe it. What kind of pastor would throw a party for a prostitute? Pastors are supposed to point fingers and shout judgment, not "Happy Birthday!" What kind of church would hire a pastor like this?

Campolo ends the story by telling him exactly what kind of church he's from. A church that worships a God, who "throws parties for prostitutes."[2]

2. Ibid., 9.

Corrie Ten Boom

IN THE LATE SPRING of 1942, an elderly man in Haarlam, Netherlands, and his two unmarried daughters, Betsie and Corrie, opened their home to a Jewish woman seeking to evade deportation to a concentration camp by the Nazis. For the next two years, the Ten Booms, who were devout Christians, sheltered and fed a constant stream of Jews seeking to escape the Nazi death camps. In 1944, they were caught and sent to the camps themselves. Corrie's father died in prison, and her sister Betsie died near the end of the war in the concentration camp Ravensbrück. Corrie was released, due to a clerical error, shortly afterward. Days after her release, all women in the camp Corrie's age were executed.

Their stories are told in Corrie's words in two small, simple, yet deeply moving books, *The Hiding Place*[1] and *A Prisoner and Yet.*[2] During their time together in the camps, the Ten Boom sisters relentlessly spoke of the love and mercy of God in these fortresses of humanity's hatred and lack of compassion.

For thirty-nine years after her release, Corrie Ten Boom traveled the world telling her story and the story of God's love for the world, made known in the life and death of Jesus. Thousands upon thousands heard her and were moved by her simple and yet radically profound message. We are loved by God. God sees our suffering and enters into it with us. Nowhere is this more true than at the cross. Again and again, those that heard her experienced forgiveness and reconciliation with God. Stories of these years are told in another book, *Tramp for the Lord.*[3]

In this book, one man who came to listen to Corrie stands out. In 1947, Corrie spoke throughout postwar Germany. She described the response there as unlike anywhere else she spoke through her life. Still overwhelmed by the violence, atrocity, and stunning defeat of the war, audiences in Germany would listen to her recount her story in total silence and would leave afterward in silence as well. Whereas in other countries

---

1. Ten Boom, *The Hiding Place.*
2. Ten Boom, *A Prisoner and Yet.*
3. Ten Boom, *Tramp for the Lord*, 55–57.

crowds would want to meet her, talk to her, or ask her to pray for them after she spoke, in the Germany of 1947, the crowds would silently leave.

One night, a middle-aged man did not get up and leave with the rest. As he enthusiastically rushed forward at the end of her talk, Ten Boom describes her response this way: "It came back with a rush: the huge room with its harsh overhead lights: the pathetic pile of shoes and dresses in the center of the floor; the shame of walking naked past this man . . . I remembered him and the leather crop swinging from his belt. I was face to face with one of my captors and my blood froze."

They began to talk, or rather the man began to talk while Corrie tried to avoid looking him in the eye. He said he too had been at Ravensbrück as a guard, confirming what she already knew. He said he had become a Christian after the war and prayed that God would forgive him for all that he had done there. He extended his hand toward Corrie and asked her to forgive him, too.

For some time, she stood there, unable to speak or reach out to take his hand. Can any of us blame her? There are people whom I have some grudge with, whom I feel have slighted or offended me somehow, whom I'd find difficult to forgive and embrace. This is a man who had taken part in the slow, brutal, and dehumanizing killing of her sister and countless others.

But she also had this thought. She already had experienced in her ministry in Holland that "those who were able to forgive their former enemies were able to return to the outside world and rebuild their lives, no matter what the physical scars. Those who nursed their bitterness remained invalids."

Completely lacking emotion, she forced herself to lift and extend her hand. As she took his hand: "An incredible thing took place. The current started in my shoulder, raced down my arm, sprang into our joined hands. And then this warmth seemed to flood my whole being, bringing tears to my eyes. "I forgive you, brother!" I cried, "With all my heart." For a long moment we grasped each other's hands, the former guard and the former prisoner. I had never known God's love so intensely as I did then."

No one would have held it against Corrie if she had concluded, "I just can't do it. I have hurt too much because of this man and those like him. I will not dishonor my sister's memory by taking his hand." In fact, some of us might feel this would be a more appropriate tack to take. A good bit of the argument made by those who support the death penalty is that victims *have a right to revenge, to retribution.* But does it work?

In recent years, behavioral scientists have conducted studies of victims of injustice from the former apartheid regime in South Africa. As discussed earlier, following the dismantling of apartheid and the election of former prisoner, Nelson Mandela, as president of South Africa, Anglican Bishop Desmond Tutu established the "Truth and Reconciliation Commission," which The studies have sought to measure the long-term emotional and psychological health of the victims. What these studies have found confirms Corrie Ten Boom's insight. Those who have been able to find some way to forgive are far healthier than those who have not. We seem to be wired with a need for reconciliation.

The Power of Downward Mobility

A T A 1988 YOUNG Life conference, which was attended by a few hundred staff and leaders, the speaker in front of the room did not look comfortable. Short, conservatively dressed, visibly shy, and clearly not comfortable with the introduction that she'd just been given, Sheila looked like she'd rather not be there. She'd been introduced as someone who had "single handedly had more impact upon a high school for Jesus than anyone in all of Young Life (a ministry with thousands of high school ministries and decades of history)."

The person who introduced her had provided this basic history before Sheila stood up. She had been a freshman at Greenhills High School in the Cincinnati suburbs when she'd gotten involved in Young Life. It was a pretty small group at the time, but Sheila had liked it and stayed involved, going to camp at the end of that school year. There, she had had a profound experience of Jesus' love and had come home passionately committed to living out this love in her life.

Before their sophomore years, she and two friends who had also gone to camp sat down and talked about what it would look like to love Greenhills High School the way they were convinced Jesus loved them. They started making a list of things they could do. None of it included things like "standing up on the cafeteria lunch tables and reading from the Bible" or "confronting people in the halls about their spiritual beliefs." Instead, the list included things like, "sit at lunch with anyone sitting by themselves," or "always give freshmen rides home when they need them," or "always let younger kids have the best seats in the car and first pick of the music on the radio." They would work their way down the social ladder of their school. It was not fancy stuff.

But, they lived it out. By the time they were seniors, in a high school of only about eight hundred students, over three hundred of them would regularly come to Young Life. Over two hundred would go to camp in the summer.

Ten years after Sheila started all of this as a high school sophomore, I happened to be at a Greenhills Young Life meeting. Afterwards, everyone (all 250!) was headed to a local fast food place to hang out. I didn't have a car, so one of the college leaders was giving me a ride. I was already in the back seat when two high school kids got in, too. One was a senior, about 6'5" and a starter on the varsity basketball team; the other was a freshmen about 5'6" and looking nervous. When they got to the car, the senior squeezed himself into the back.

"What are you doing?" asked the freshman. "I ought to take the back."

"No problem. I like it better back here. Why don't you take the front and, hey, why don't you pick your favorite radio station?"

At the pizza place, I asked the senior, "Hey, why'd you take the backseat?" My expectation was going to be that he'd say something like, "Well, our leaders tell us we are supposed to do that, so I did."

Instead, he said, "I don't know. When I was a freshmen, the seniors always let me sit up front and pick the music and that just made me feel really cool, so now I try to do the same thing."

"Again Jesus asked, 'What shall I compare the kingdom of God to?
It is like yeast that a woman took and mixed into a large amount of flour
until it had worked its way through the dough.'"
—Luke 13:20–21

Gettysburg, Fifty Years Later

IN HIS BOOK, *THE Longing for Home*, Frederick Buechner tells of a moment in Ken Burns's PBS series, "The Civil War." The Battle of Gettysburg, fought over three days in July of 1893, saw more casualties, almost fifty thousand, than any other single battle of the Civil War. It has achieved lasting fame from Abraham Lincoln's "Gettysburg Address," given at the site a few months after the battle.

In Burns's series, a story is told of a re-enactment of the battle held on its fiftieth anniversary in 1913. Civil War enthusiasts re-enact battles all the time, but this re-enactment featured the survivors of both the Confederate and Union armies that had actually fought in the battle five decades earlier. The most famous moment in this most famous battle was Pickett's charge. Pickett, a Confederate officer, led a charge of his troops up a hill only to see them cut down by the Union forces at the top of the hill. This charge was the turning part of the battle and, many say, of the entire war. Here is how Buechner describes the scene in 1913: "As the old men among the rocks began to rush down at the old men coming across the field, a great cry went up, only instead of doing battle as they had half a century earlier, this time they threw their arms around each other. They embraced each other and openly wept."[1]

"For Jesus himself is our peace, who has made the two one and destroyed the barrier, the dividing wall of hostility."
—Ephesians 2:14

---

1. Buechner, *The Longing for Home*, 137.

Finding Faith in Unexpected Places

IN HIS WONDERFUL BOOK *Soul Survivor,*[1] Philip Yancey profiles the renowned Pulitzer Prize winning psychiatrist and oral historian, Robert Coles. In the early 1960s, Coles was a Harvard, Columbia, and University of Chicago trained pediatrician and psychiatrist who was also an agnostic, a heavy drinker, and mildly to significantly depressed. He was working for the Air Force in Mississippi. One day, driving through New Orleans, he was stopped in traffic by a barricade set up by Louisiana state troopers. There was a race riot going on.

What was the cause of the riot? Six-year-old Ruby Bridges, an African-American girl, was going to school. He discovered that this was the scene every day as she went to school, a school where all of the other students, white students, were being kept home by their parents to protest her presence at *their* school.

Already interested in studying the ways in which children cope with stress, Coles decided he'd found a perfect subject. What kid could be under more stress than Ruby? He spoke with the family, and over time was granted permission to interview her.

He asked Ruby how she got through the walks to the school with all of the adults yelling at her and calling her names. She said that she prayed. Well, what did she pray for?

She prayed for herself and, she said, she prayed for the white adults she encountered every day. She prayed that God would forgive them. Because that is what Jesus had done. He had prayed for his enemies, asking God to forgive them.

Ruby was the first of what became dozens of African-American children whom Coles interviewed during the years of school integration in the South. Over and over again, he encountered the same thing: tiny, frail, deeply vulnerable children who prayed for the adults who hated them and yelled at them. Children who said they had strength to keep showing up for the walk to school because that's what Jesus would have done. That was the kind of thing Jesus did.

---

1. Yancey, *Soul Survivor*, 87–118.

Coles, who had all the academic answers to coping with stress, dealing with anger, and developing healthy self-esteem, had no categories for what he encountered in these kids. He had never met anyone like them.

He was an avid reader and began to read spiritual classics and Christian authors. He got involved with the Civil Rights Movement and came to see the faith of many of the adults, like Martin Luther King, that fueled their passion for justice. But nothing touched him or drew him toward faith like these children.

Robert Coles, intellectual giant and academic celebrity, became a Christian. His tutors in faith, his mentors, were impoverished African-American grade school children, children who understood that they were loved by God and that, therefore, they could have the courage to love those who hated them and wished them harm. They changed his life. They and others liked them set in motion events that changed and continue to change America.

A Stunned Crowd at the Sundance Film Festival

RECONCILIATION AND EMBRACE DO not always require agreement or the absence of difference. My most profound experience of this took place in Park City, Utah, in January of 2006. My wife, Elizabeth, and I were part of a group of theology students and faculty from Fuller Theological Seminary who attended a unique "classroom" experience at the Sundance Film Festival. Sundance is one of the most prestigious independent film festivals in the world. Every January, throngs of people descend upon the resort town of Park City and watch hundreds of independent films premier during the week long festival. The movies range from documentaries to dramas and from the relatively traditional to the extravagantly bizarre.

In the middle of this week-long carnival of film watching, several dozen Christians from Fuller attended several films each day and then talked about them in a local church or in pubs around town. It was a fascinating experience, hosted by Fuller professor and veteran of the Hollywood film industry, Craig Detwieler.

Easily the most memorable experience of the week for my wife and me occurred at the morning screening of a film at a local elementary school. The film was a drama set in the southern United States in a largely Christian, church-going community. The family at the center of the film has an enlightening experience early in the film, and they leave their uptight, rigid, Christian personas and begin to embrace their sexuality in free and open ways. This shocks and offends their entire community. The Christians eventually kill most of the family. The film dealt with Christian hostilities to sexuality on several levels, including homosexuality.

At Sundance, after each screening, the director and perhaps some of the others involved in the movie, come up for a question-and-answer period with the audience. The applause is always warm and the questions interesting. After this film, the director came up and the room erupted. It was like Bono or Michael Jordan had walked into the room.

Once the standing ovation subsided, the questions and statements began. A lot of them were along these lines: "Thank you for making this film! It is about time some one told the truth about the Christians and stuck it to them!" These comments were greeted with more thunderous applause. "It's a shame Christians will never watch this film, but somebody needs to force them to so they can see how horrible they are."

Gay men stood up and, in tears, said, "I grew up in the Church and experienced so much pain there. Thank you for telling my story." The director shared that this had been his experience. His dad had been a Sunday School teacher who got booted from his role because the kids in his class laughed too much. He and his family never went back. One of the cast members shared that she was a Christian and that many of her family members and Christian friends had stopped talking to her because of her role in the film.

And then Craig Detwieller, the teacher of our course, stood up. He began by complimenting the director on various elements of the film, but quickly moved into more personal ground. "I'm from North Carolina, just like the characters in this movie and just like you [the director]. I am who you made this movie about. I am an evangelical Christian. In fact I'm here at Sundance with a bunch of seminary students from a school in California." You could hear the air go out of the room as everyone waited for him to unload. That's what virtually everyone expected.

And then Craig started to cry. And then he said, "You made a movie that honestly speaks about how so many people, and particularly people in the gay community, feel about how they've been treated by the Church. I want to apologize. I want you to know that I am sorry for everything I or others have done to wound you."

Nobody really had much more to say after that. The question and answer session wrapped up, and some folks began to leave. But a lot of folks, from the cast and production team of the movie and from the audience, wanted to talk to Craig. Many of us from Fuller got swept into the conversations as well.

At one point, my wife and I ended up talking to one of the actors from the film who happened to be gay. Midway through our conversation, he started crying. "I'm okay," he said. "I've just never believed there was a world where people like you wouldn't hate me."

One of the fascinating aspects of those thirty minutes or so of discussion that followed Craig's comments was that no one seemed interested in making points. If anything, the folks from the movie went out of their way to say, "Hey, I know why you feel the Bible tells you that you can't affirm me. I'm just so thankful that you understand that that hurts. It means so much to me to know that you care about me." Conversely, many of the folks from Fuller were able to say, "I *do* think the Bible has things to say about sexuality that matter, but I also think it has a lot to say about being loving and gentle, and the Church has done a pretty awful job of being either. I want to apologize for that."

Many of the folks that talked to Craig or the students in attendance relayed similar stories. They had grown up in the Church. They had known they were gay for as long as they could remember. They struggled with it for years. They had come out in late high school, in college, or as adults. They had been summarily rejected by all of the Christians they knew as soon as they did. Most of them spoke of aching to experience God like they had growing up. Most of them spoke with more sadness than anger at the hostile and cruel things that had been said and done to them by Christians. One after another of them hugged Craig or others of us, and we all wept.

The very large issues of faith and sexuality were not resolved that day. But, for everyone there, Christians and members of the gay community alike, it was the first time that the prospect of dialoging about those issues with friends rather than enemies seemed possible. It seemed like, perhaps, a way could be found forward that was not characterized by vitriol, sarcasm, and rejection.

Perhaps, *shalom* might find a way after all.

A Disappointing Season

I WAS RUNNING ON a road around Saranac Lake in upstate New York (about fifteen miles from Lake Placid, the site of the 1980 Winter Olympics) with two high school kids, a guy and a girl. We were all spending a month working at a Young Life camp there. They were high school runners needing to stay in shape, and I coached cross-country back home, so I need to run as well. We were chatting as we ran. I'd just asked them how the previous year had been for them from a running standpoint.

The girl, Karen, replied, "It was a hugely disappointing season. Very discouraging."

I shifted into coach mode. "Did you not hit the times you wanted or place as high at State as you had the year before? You know, that could be all kinds of things. Overtraining. Low iron. A growth spurt."

"No, actually, I ran way better than I had my freshman and sophomore years. I placed in the top ten at the State cross-country meet and set a school record in track. That wasn't the problem at all. What was so disappointing was that, after both my freshman and sophomore years, I'd gotten eight to ten girls on the team to come with me to camp. My sophomore year, we had a team Bible study all year, even in the off-season. This year, I was so focused on my personal running goals, I never got the Bible study started, and only one girl from the team came to camp this year."

My orientation had been just like everyone else's typically would be. What defined success? Success was winning. It was achieving personal glory. Karen had an altogether different perspective. If anything, her personal success had become an obstacle to reaching out to her friends.

Now, I suspect she was being a bit too hard on herself and probably loved her teammates well, even as she accomplished a great deal personally. What impressed me, though, was that at seventeen she would even think that way. I was thirty, and that wasn't the way I thought.

Not *Either/Or* but *Both And*

I N THE EARLY 1980S, a few teenagers in Ireland were coming alive to Jesus and the Christian faith. They were also interested in music and formed a band with one of their friends. In the early years of their band, they received a lot of advice from their Christian community that they should focus their music and their time on personal spiritual growth instead of achieving rock stardom. Their community was worried that they would get swallowed up by "the world" and lose their faith. The band's early music reflects the personal faith of the band's lead singer and songwriter. Young Christians in America hailed them as, finally, a hip, commercially credible, and successful "Christian band."

For a few years after their initial success with overtly Christian music, it looked like the community's concerns were well founded. The band released a few albums and went on tours that certainly did not look or sound particularly "Christian." In fact, the band's tour persona seemed to almost mock or parody its previous Christian image. Fans, many of whom had been drawn to the band because of their overtly Christian lyrics, were dismayed and confused.

Then, in 2000, the band released a new album that again spoke stirringly about spiritual issues from a squarely Christian perspective. The closing song on the album was literally an explication of the Christian doctrine of grace. As they embarked upon the tour for this album, the band's leader often prayed or quoted scripture in front of the audience. The band, of course, was U2, the lead singer Bono, and the album was *All That You Can't Leave Behind.*[1]

What was fascinating about U2's resurgence into publicly displayed Christian faith was the additional message that now accompanied it. Bono, the band's front man, wasn't interested in just talking about Jesus, the savior of souls. He wanted to talk, passionately and insistently, about a Jesus who was concerned with global poverty and justice. U2 concerts became one part rock concert, one part worship experience, and a generous part global issues tutorial and motivational lecture.

1. U2, *All That You Can't Leave Behind.*

In February of 2006, Bono was invited to speak at the President's National Prayer Breakfast in Washington, DC. His talk was about the biblical Year of Jubilee and its implications for present-day issues of disease, hunger, and economic justice. He has, along with others, formed the One Campaign, a multi-organizational attempt to eradicate global extreme poverty.

U2 seems to have discovered a truth that has tended to get lost to most Christians in the West. Some Christians believe that Jesus came to feed the hungry, clothe the poor, and heal the sick. Some in this group feel that talk of Jesus saving souls is a distraction from Jesus' real ministry, saving bodies right now from societal ills. This is often called the *Social Gospel*. On the other side, are Christians who answer the question, "Why did Jesus come to earth?" very quickly, confidently, and differently. "He came to die on the cross for the forgiveness of my sins so I can go to heaven when I die." Both sides have tended to look suspiciously or negatively at the other.

As Bono sings songs about the doctrine of grace and pleads with the wealthy West to mobilize to address global issues of poverty, disease, and justice, he is rejecting a vision that sees these two versions of Christianity as either/or. He is demanding that we see them as both/and. He is admonishing us to realize that, while the Bible talks extensively about Jesus coming to save us from our sins, it also talks about the needs of the poor more than any other topic, speaking about it over three thousand times. He is standing beside the Apostle Paul who wrote, "If anyone is in Christ, the new creation has come; The old has gone, the new is here! All this is from God who was reconciling the world to himself through Christ and gave us the ministry of reconciliation."[2]

I have emphasized a few phrases in this passage from 2 Corinthians to make my point. Is Jesus about saving souls, reconciling us to God? You bet. Absolutely. Is Jesus about saving *all* the world, *all* creation? Yes. Jesus is about that too.

Is Matthew right when Jesus in his version of the Sermon on the Mount, says, "Blessed are the poor *in spirit*," symbolizing our spiritual need for forgiveness from sins, or should we side with Luke, who has Jesus saying, "Blessed are the poor," period? Who is right, Matthew or Luke? My response is *yes, Both* are right. We, all of us, need to wake up to our

2. 2 Corinthians 5:18.

spiritual poverty, and we also need to be awakened to the literal poverty in the world around us and the part we play in causing it and can play in eliminating it.

As Bono has become deeply engaged in speaking about personal faith *and* social engagement to transform the world, he has not invented a new paradigm; it only seems that way if you listen to Christians squabble with each other. Throughout history, there have been Christians who have seen the same both/and, personal salvation hand in hand with social justice. It was Christians, first in England and later in America, who called their nations (ostensibly Christian nations) to wake up to the evils of slavery. It was the British missionary Paul Brand who labored to discover the causes of leprosy and brought relief to those ravaged by that disease. It was Mother Theresa who brought God's message of grace and love to the poorest of the poor in Calcutta. The list could go on and on. All believed deeply in salvation from sin and life everlasting. They also all believed passionately in bringing the goodness of the Kingdom of God to a world in desperate need of it right now. Earlier we talked about righteousness as *tsedeqah*, things being in right relation, things being "as they should be." The Gospel is always about taking "that which should not be," both personal sin *and* global injustice, and turning it into *tsedeqah,* that which should be.

A Gospel that only does good deeds for the poor is incomplete. Likewise, a Gospel that only focuses upon personal salvation and personal forgiveness from sin is missing a huge part of the message of Jesus. Not *either/or*, but *both/and*.

Bono Talks About the Difference
Between Grace and Karma

I<small>N</small> 2005, M<small>ITCHKA</small> A<small>SSAYAS</small> published a long and wandering book of lengthy interviews he had conducted with U2's Bono. The book is more than 370 pages long; Bono is not shy. Among the many things they talked about were Jesus and Christianity. As many are, Assayas is very dubious about the good of religious belief in the world. Having seen a lot of bad done in the name of Christianity or Islam or any number of religions, he, like much of the modern world, is at best skeptical and often hostile to the idea that belief in God can lead to anything good. As part of a discussion about that, about two-thirds of the way through the book, Bono begins talking about grace versus karma. Assayas is confused and asks him to clarify what in the world he is talking about. This is how Bono replies:

> You see, at the center of all religions is the idea of Karma. You know, what you put out comes back to you: an eye for an eye, a tooth for a tooth, or in physics—in physical laws—every action is meet by an equal or an opposite one. It's clear to me that Karma is at the very heart of the Universe. I'm absolutely sure of it. And yet, along comes this idea called Grace to upend all that "you reap, so will you sow" stuff. Love interrupts, if you like the consequences of your actions, which in my case is very good news indeed, because I've done a lot of stupid stuff . . . I'd be in big trouble if Karma was going to finally be my judge. I'd be in deep shit. It doesn't excuse my mistakes, but I'm holding out for Grace. I'm holding out that Jesus took my sins onto the Cross . . .[1]

On that 2000 album, *All That You Can't Leave Behind,* that seemed to mark, for many listeners at least, the "return" of Bono and U2 talking openly about Christian faith (the band themselves and many discerning fans would say they had always continued the conversation, just, for awhile, somewhat ironically), the band ended the album with the song, "Grace." It is a beautiful song, a melody much like a lullaby, that contrasts the theological concept of Grace with a little girl whose name is Grace. The song talks about Grace's ability to see goodness and beauty where

1. Assayas, *Bono,* 226.

others see only ugliness. It talks about Grace's ability to bring healing and to literally change everything.

Bono: International rock star, leader of worldwide social justice movements, and a singer of lullabies to the concept of Grace.

How Wide Is God's Embrace?

THIS CHAPTER MAKES ME more anxious than anything else in the book. I've got friends for whom *the* most significant obstacle to participating in the Christian faith is their frustration with what feels to them to be its arrogant exclusivity. Basically they say, "I don't think I can believe in a religion or a God who is fine with the vast majority of humanity going to hell for all eternity." On the other hand, I've got friends for whom one of the most worrisome heretical charges one can make is to accuse someone of *universalism,* or the idea that God will save everyone.

My problem? I feel the concerns of both groups. I worry along with my questioning friends if the Gospel really can be called Good News if it is not good news for the vast, vast majority of all humanity. At the same time, I also believe that the story of God in the Bible is pretty clear that the only hope for humanity, individually or collectively, is through God's gracious actions toward us in Jesus. I don't think all roads lead to heaven. So what am I to do? Where do others of us who might have one or both of the same concerns turn?

The church that I grew up in took a very narrow view of this. Not only were all those outside of a specifically Christian response excluded, but most who thought they were Christians were excluded as well. Only those who were baptized in a very specific way, worshipped in very specific ways, and understood the Bible just as we did had any hope of being saved. Once in seventh-grade Sunday School, I asked the teacher, "But what about the thief on the cross? He wasn't baptized as an adult, nor do we know that he avoided instrumental music in church, but Jesus says he's going to heaven." I didn't get an answer, and my parents got chided for having a disrespectful son.

As I pointed out in an earlier piece, while I soon left behind that narrow definition of how salvation was accessed, I didn't broaden my view by much. My interaction with John on the lawn at Young Life camp, trying to argue him out of his confidence in his Christian background and into the formulaic response of my construction, proves that. As has time has gone by since, that instance and others have troubled me.

Here is where I have landed over the last several years of doing ministry. Here is what I might say when sitting in a circle with a group of high school kids on the trail in Colorado or sitting in the dining commons at George Fox University having coffee with a student. I believe hell is real. I believe it is possible to say "no" to the embrace of God. I also believe that is what we have to do—say "no." To me, that is different than believing heaven is available only to those who clearly say "yes" right now in ways we can easily point to. (I feel your heresy meter revving up; please hang with me.)

I think this for a few biblical reasons. The first is what feels to me to be the overwhelming flow or thread running through scripture. God just seems to again and again find the lost, rescue the helpless, and bring life to the barren. Yes, there are times of judgment to be found in the Bible, but the Psalmist often talks about mercies that endure forever. It seems possible to get lost, to cut oneself off from God, but the more I read the story of God, it seems pretty hard to do.

In 1 Corinthians, Paul says, "Death where is your victory? Death, where is your sting?"[1] It is gone. "Death has been swallowed up in victory." [2]This is what the resurrection accomplishes. We are no longer prisoners to death. But we all still die, right? So what does this mean? Certainly, part of what it means that we are no longer certain of spiritual death. We have the possibility and even the promise of salvation. But why does Paul talk so much about physical death here if what all he really means is salvation?

From a spiritual standpoint, what is the power that physical death has over us? It ends the possibility of repentance. A young woman might have attended church camp and been deeply moved by the message of God's grace spoken there. But she still had questions and did not respond. Sitting on the bus headed home, not interacting with the others because she's deep in thought about what she has heard, she doesn't see the approaching semi, driver asleep at the wheel, as it plows head on into her bus. Killed instantly in the ensuing ball of flame, has death claimed victory over her? Is she a soul who, had she had a few more minutes, might have responded to grace, but because the semi got there first, did not? Is she now immediately ushered into hell? Is her eternal destiny changed by the timing of the out-of-control truck?

I believe part of the resurrection destroying the sting and victory of death is that all is not lost for this young woman. Response to Christ is

1. 1 Corinthians 15:35.
2. 2 Corinthians 15:34.

still her only hope for salvation, but I don't believe the semi truck ended it. I fully recognize that this is not a position held by anywhere close to most evangelical Christians. I fully recognize that I may be wrong in this, but a couple of passages from scripture have been part of what has brought me to this belief.

The first is a familiar story, Jesus' parable of the sheep and the goats.[3] In this parable, people come before Jesus after their deaths and are either welcomed into paradise or not. Those welcomed are the sheep and those rejected are goats. The irony of the parable, of course, is that those who come thinking they are sheep turn out to be goats. Jesus says to them, "I was thirsty and you didn't give me anything to drink. I was hungry and you didn't feed me." They protest that this isn't fair. When did they have an opportunity to do this? Jesus replies, "Whenever you did not do this for the least of these, you did not do it for me." In essence, you thought you were followers of me, but your lack of care or concern for your fellow humans shows otherwise.

In contrast, a group comes before him, and they are welcomed. The mirror opposite of the previous dialogue follows. They claim, "We never fed you, gave you anything to drink, clothed you." Jesus replies that, though they did not know it, their care and compassion for others were really care for him, and they are welcomed into paradise.

A few points in this parable seem worth noting. First, it is Jesus and how one cares for or responds to him that is of vital importance. This is not universalism. The arms of embrace are Jesus', and it is to him that we must respond. Second, the second group, the sheep, seemed to have not in a conscious way known of or responded to Jesus during their lives. They appear before Jesus after death and protest that there must be some mistake; they had not knowingly acted for Jesus during their lives. But, somehow, Jesus knows that they would have, or considers their acts of mercy to be directed toward him. Finally, all of this happens after they have all died. There's no formula here or declaration that individuals can respond to Jesus after death, but it is a provocative story, and Jesus tells it. I am not suggesting that personal faith in Jesus in this life is unimportant, but this parable seems to suggest that perhaps God is not as limited as many of us have supposed in finding those who would have faith in God.

3. Matthew 25:31–46.

1 Peter contains an even more cryptic and strange passage. It starts normally enough; in fact, this part is quoted often, "For Christ suffered once for our sins, the righteous for the unrighteous, to bring you to God. He was put to death in the body but made alive in the Spirit."[4] Absolutely. This is consistent with everything else in the story of scripture and is at the heart of traditional Christian belief. But then these are the very next verses that follow. "In that state he went and made proclamation to the imprisoned spirits—to those who were disobedient long ago when God waited patiently in the days of Noah while the ark was being built."[5]

Well, that part doesn't get quoted very much. Where is this place that souls from the days of Noah, when the earth was so wicked that God destroyed everyone other than Noah and his family, get imprisoned? It would be safe to assume that they are imprisoned in hell. And Christ, in some way, comes to them, *in hell* and *preaches to them.* Theologians have argued a great deal about what this means, and it is one verse and is one instance, but it seems to me that at least once, *souls who had been wicked in life, judged by God in death, and sent to hell are preached to and that, in this one instance, it seems like hell was not necessarily final.* In saying that, I'm not saying that these souls didn't still need to respond in some way, to repent, to actively welcome this opportunity. It is conceivable that, even in hell, they may not have. I am also not saying that this passage proves in any way that this happens more than once.

I am saying that when I read the story of the Bible, with God's relentless pursuit of reconciliation, and when I read these stories that seem to speak of, at least in these cases, our earthly life not being the limit of the opportunity of God's love to find us, I have hope that this extends beyond these isolated examples. I still believe that Christ alone can reconcile us to the Triune God. All roads do not lead to God. I also believe, in the end, that embrace can be resisted. It is possible for the older son to remain outside the party, arms crossed on the porch, no matter how the father pleads with him to come in. I do believe, or at least strongly hope, that this embrace is made available to more of us than we have tended to think.

I recognize that any number of you reading this will not find this position acceptable. Some will feel like it really is just "universalism in sheep's clothing," an example of trying to have it both ways—be a universalist and

4. 1 Peter 3:18.
5. 1 Petet 3:19–20.

still believe that Jesus exclusively saves. In my heart, that's not what I think I am doing, but I know I won't convince some of that. On the other hand, some will feel that to claim that "the arms of God's embrace that extend to us are Jesus' and his alone" is too exclusive. This group wants a God who unconditionally accepts all. To that group, I have a couple of responses.

Both of my responses to the claim of exclusivism have their basis in the nature of relationships. The entire flow of the book, and I believe the entire flow of God's story in scripture, is that we are specifically desired by the relational God. Just as we are specifically desired, the one who desires us is specific. Is it really the same thing to say, "I value love, so I'll marry you"? One object of love is as good as another, and anyone will do," as opposed to, "You. You are the one I love and desire to marry. Of all others, you are the one I love"? God loves us specifically like that and asks that in return. That's not God being arrogant or exclusive. Is the bride that says, "Love me. Love me uniquely and exclusively, for that is how I love you," being arrogant?

Also, do we really want all to be accepted unconditionally? We want that for ourselves, certainly. We want it for the children we see starving on television. We want that for those battered and scarred by life. But do we want that for their abusers? Do we want a God that could say to a pedophile, a rapist, a Hitler, "I don't care at all about all that; just give me a hug"? We believe, at least in our better moments, in forgiveness. We also want things to be put right, for justice to be done. Namely, the embrace of Hosea is the offer for Gomer to now be his wife, not to continue being a prostitute. The embrace of the father is for the prodigal son to come home, not to continue to rebel in a far off land. If the state of one's heart is that it would not or will not enter into all that a relationship with God entails—loving God and joining God in the work of the Kingdom—the embrace cannot happen. I believe any who would welcome that embrace and the relationship offered in it will have it. I don't believe that is any-where near all of us. But I sure think there will be a lot more of us than I thought when I was younger.

Heart Parties

I HAVE TWO DELIGHTFUL daughters, Bailey and Rachel. They laugh all the time and love to draw, ride bikes, have "family wrestle" (a post-dinner tradition in our house), and most other things that kids in first and second grade like. Bailey, our oldest, is particularly creative and emotional sensitive *and* may well have a borderline case of Asperger's Syndrome. While that causes minimal problems for her these days, when she was younger, it made life quite challenging. Until she was six, social interaction with peers was difficult, and she did not have friends her age other than her sister.

When she was four, we lived in Iowa City where Elizabeth and I worked with Young Life, which meant that there were a lot of high school and college aged kids in the girls' lives. Soon after Christmas that year, Bailey somehow became aware that Valentine's Day was the next major holiday. She didn't know the name of it, but she was sure it involved hearts.

She announced, "I want to have a heart party." We asked her who she wanted to invite to the heart party, and she said the Otterbein children, two older kids from our church that she knew because we were friends with their parents. They were both more than four years older than Bailey, so we weren't quite sure how this heart party thing was going to go, but she was determined.

In fact, she began making "cards for the heart party." This involved taking pink, red, or white pieces of construction paper and drawing a heart on them, folding them, and putting them in a pile with the other cards. Simple enough. Except that Bailey, over the next month or so, made a *lot* of cards. She would make from a few to more than a dozen a day, and they really started to pile up. With the pile, up rose her expectations for this party. "I can't wait for the heart party, Dad. It's going to be great!"

Well, her mom and I weren't so sure. The Otterbein kids were nice enough, but they were quite a bit older than Bailey and, given all the things that complicated life for Bailey, she wasn't super adept at sustaining social interactions in the first place. We had real concerns that her massive expectations were going to come crashing into this awkward social reality, and that it was going to be very painful for her. Plus, we were concerned that this would be the first taste of what, we assumed at the time, quite a bit of her life would look like.

Like I said, we had a lot of college aged folks in our lives due to our Young Life involvement in this university town, and all of them knew our girls. They'd all seen the pile of "heart cards" growing on our living room bookshelf. A couple of times, I'd talked with a few of the guys about my anxiety about the upcoming party.

The day came, and sure enough, it was just as awkward as anticipated. The Otterbein kids definitely had the look of kids whose parents had forced them to come. Perhaps the bribe of cake and ice cream at the end had been enough to get them there. Bailey, as usual, had very specific ideas about what games ought to be played and how the party should proceed, but being both four and a kid with some challenges, she did not have much ability to communicate those things. We were counting the minutes until we could get to the cake and ice cream and bring the heart party to an end. Elizabeth and I were just hoping for minimal emotional damage.

And then the doorbell rang. Before we could get to the door, in burst three of the college aged guys who worked with us in Young Life: J. J., Jeff, and Brendon.

"Hey! We're looking for a heart party! Does anyone know where a heart party is going on?!"

"Here. We're having a heart party," Bailey said.

"That's awesome, because we love heart parties, and this looks like a great one!"

For the next hour, these three guys literally turned our living room upside down with their energy and enthusiasm. They gave piggy-back rides. They chased kids. They wrestled with them. They made up balloon games. Everything happened with a level of energy and a volume beyond belief! Everyone was literally dripping with sweat.

The Otterbein kids, who both had looked a little wary and hesitant when the guys burst into the room, were swept away into the enthusiasm. Within minutes, they were laughing and playing with these guys like they were much younger kids. My two daughters were beside themselves with joy. They squealed, laughed, and screamed until they literally fell to the ground in exhaustion.

It was the most beautiful thing I'd ever seen. Bailey would, and still will, even though her social skills are infinitely more up to speed now than they were then, have plenty of awkward social experiences. She will have times when life is not kind.

But not this day!

On this day, her weeks and weeks of preparations and expectations were totally eclipsed by the reality. Her heart party was better than even she could have dreamed!

For an hour, *shalom* invaded our house.

The Kingdom of God took up residence at 309 Amhurst Street in Iowa City, Iowa. Bailey was vulnerable and awkward. Three twenty-one-year-old guys saw that and intervened. They loved Bailey. They loved our whole family and, because of that, they gave us a great gift.

The Kingdom of God is a lot of things, and it's a very few things. In many ways, it is nothing more than this: Throwing heart parties. God throwing them for us, through the cross, through the embrace of grace. And, it's us throwing heart parties for others. Seeing people in need and loving them extravagantly, because that is what Jesus has done for us. Jesus talked about banquets. Israel anticipated the Year of Jubilee. Jesus told stories of great celebrations at the finding of lost sheep, lost coins, and lost children. It's not hard to be an ambassador of the Kingdom. Just throw a heart party!

Ultimately, any heart party we throw, any moment where we create a glimpse of *shalom* here on earth is but that: a glimpse. The reality of what is to come is infinitely better. We were made for this. We were created to know and experience the wonderful relationality of God. We have, through our rebellion, lost that experience. The story of God is the restoration of that. Actually, restoration is hardly the right word. It seems to imply patching a leaky tire or putting a patch on a torn pair of pants. What God's embrace of humanity—through the cross of Jesus, his resurrection, and the ongoing work of those who know and follow him—is about is "making all things new."

It is to be welcomed home. It is to find that, though we've been crouching in alleyways all our lives, there is a seat at the Banquet for us. It is to join in the adventure of bringing the world to this feast of *shalom*. It is to melt into the healing, forgiving, life-giving arms of God, to feel God's heart race with joy as we hear whispered to us, "Welcome home! I have missed you so!"

The Banquet/The Heart Party by Andrew Watson, 2008

J. J., Bailey, and Rachel at the Heart Party

The Heart Party

The Banquet/The Heart Party by Andrew Watson, 2008

J. J., Bailey, and Rachel at the Heart Party

The Heart Party

Bibliography

Alberhasky, J. J. "Good Advice." From the album *Only the Bony*. Iowa City, IA: Self-released, 2006.

Alexander, Cecil Frances. "There Is a Green Hill Far Away." In *Hymns for Little Children*, 1848.

Alexander, James W. "O Sacred Head Now Wounded," 1830.

Assayas, Michka. *Bono: In Conversation with Michka Assayas*. New York: Berkley Publishing, 2005.

Bailey, Kenneth. *The Cross and the Prodigal*. St. Louis, MO: Concordia Publishing, 1973.

Buber, Martin. *I and Thou*. New York: Scribner & Sons, 1923.

Buechner, Frederick. *The Longing for Home*. San Francisco, CA: HarperSanFrancisco, 1996.

———. "The Truth of Stories." In *The Clown in the Belfry*, 131–37. San Francisco, CA: HarperSanFrancisco, 1992.

Campolo, Tony. *The Kingdom of God Is a Party*. Nashville, TN: Thomas Nelson, 1992.

Chalke, Steve and Alan Mann. *The Lost Message of Jesus*. Grand Rapids, MI: Zondervan, 2003.

Einstein, Albert. Quoted on thinkexist.com. Online: http://en.thinkexist.com/search/searchquotation.asp?search=It+is+strange+to+be+so+known+so+universally+and+yet+be+so+lonely

Eliot, T. S. *Complete Poems and Plays: 1909–1950*. New York, NY: Harcourt, 1952.

Empson, William. Quoted by Eric Griffiths in "William Empson's Fixated Faith," *The Times Literary Supplement*, October 24, 2007. Online: http://entertainment.timesonline.co.uk/tol/arts_and_entertainment/the_tls/article2730351.ece, paragraph 5.

Huxley, Aldoux. Quoted by Dallas Willard, The *Divine Conspiracy: Rediscovering Our Hidden Life in God*. New York, NY: HarperCollins, 1998.

Lewis, C. S. *Mere Christianity*. New York: Harper Collins, 1952.

———. *Surprised by Joy*. New York: Harcourt Brace, 1955.

———. "Transposition." In *The Weight of Glory*. Grand Rapids, MI: Eerdmans Publishing, 1966.

McLaren, Brian D. *Everything Must Change*. Nashville, TN: Thomas Nelson, 2007.

Mother Teresa of Calcutta, quoted on thinkexist.com. Online: http://en.thinkexist.com/quotation/the_most_terrible_poverty_is_loneliness_and_the/216333.html

Nouwen, Henri. Quoted by Rueben P. Job and Norman Shawchuck, *A Guide to Prayer*. Nashville, TN: The Upper Room, 1983.

Owens, Pricilla J. "Jesus Saves." In *Songs of Songs of Redeeming Love* by John R. Sweney, C. C. McCabe, Tullius C. O'Kane, and William Kirkpatrick, 1882.

Peck, M. Scott. *People of the Lie*. New York, NY: Simon & Schuster, 1983.

Percy, Walker. *Lost in the Cosmos*. New York, NY: Farrar & Straus, 1983.

———. *The Message in a Bottle*. New York, NY: Farrar & Straus, 1975.

Polanyi, Michael. *Personal Knowledge*. Chicago, IL: University of Chicago Press, 1958.

Russell, Bertrand. *Mysticism and Logic*. London, UK: Longman, 1919.

Ten Boom, Corrie. *The Hiding Place*. New York, NY: Random House, 1982.

———. *A Prisoner and Yet*. Fort Washington, PA: Christian Literature Crusade, 1954.

Bibliography

————. *Tramp for the Lord*. Fort Washington, PA: Christian Literature Crusade, 1974.

Thielicke, Helmut. *The Waiting Father*. New York, NY: Harper & Row, 1959.

Thoreau, Henry David. *Walden*, annotated edition. New Haven, CT: Yale University Press, 2004.

Tutu, Desmond. *No Future Without Forgiveness*. New York, NY: Random House, 1999.

U2. *All That You Can't Leave Behind*. Island Records, 2000.

Volf, Miroslav. *Exclusion and Embrace,* Nashville, TN: Abingdon Press, 1996.

Watts, Isaac. "When I Survey the Wondrous Cross," *Hymns and Spiritual Songs*, 1707.

Wright, N. T. *Simply Christian*. San Francisco: HarperSanFrancisco, 2006.

Yancey, Philip. *Soul Survivor*. New York: Doubleday, 2001.